The Inı

...to the North .

Mark Reid

The complete and unique guide
to a circular walk in the North York Moors

InnWay Publications

The Inn Way...to the North York Moors
© Mark Reid 2000

First Edition November 2000
Reprinted 2003 and 2006

Second Edition March 2010

A catalogue record for this book is available from the British Library.
British Library Cataloguing in Publication Data.

All maps within this publication are based upon Ordnance Survey mapping
reproduced by permission of Ordnance Survey on behalf of The Controller of Her
Majesty's Stationery Office. (c) Crown Copyright, Licence Number: 100011978

The contents of this publication are believed correct at time of copyright.
Nevertheless the author can not accept responsibility for errors and omissions, or for
changes in details given. The information contained within this publication is
intended only as a general guide.

**This is a long distance walk that, in some places, crosses remote and rough
terrain with open moorland and steep sections. Navigation may be difficult
across the high moors in poor weather; OS maps and compass essential.
Walking and outdoor activities can be strenuous and individuals must ensure
that they have suitable outdoor clothing, footwear, provisions, equipment, maps
and are suitably fit before starting the walk; inexperienced walkers should be
supervised. You are responsible for your own safety and for others in your care, so
be prepared for the unexpected - make sure you are fully equipped for the hills.**

'The Inn Way' is a Registered Trademark of Mark Reid.

Published by:
INNWAY PUBLICATIONS
102 LEEDS ROAD
HARROGATE
HG2 8HB

ISBN: 978-1-902001-17-3

www.innway.co.uk

The Inn Way

...to the North York Moors

The complete and unique guide to a circular walk in the North York Moors.

✦

The Inn Way...to the North York Moors is an 89 mile (143 km) circular walk divided into six stages. Detailed maps, route descriptions, fascinating historical quotations, snippets and pieces of information will help guide you through this wonderful moorland landscape of heather-clad ridges and green, wooded valleys, passing no less than 31 traditional English pubs and leaving you with a deeper knowledge and understanding of the North York Moors.

The Hare Inn, Scawton

For my two children, Ewan and Isla

Thou who hast given me eyes to see,
And love this sight so fair,
Give me a heart to find out Thee,
And read Thee everywhere.

(J. Keble)

Thank you to Bernadette and Stewart Reid, Rachel Gospel, Geoff Temperton, Matthew Hunt, Peter Moore, Matthew Perry, Richard Teasdale, Patrick and James Green for being my walking companions whilst researching the route for the First Edition between 1998 and 2000. Thank you to the many thousands of people who have walked the route since.

I am extremely grateful to the following organisations who have helped with my research:
English Heritage, Forest Enterprise, North Yorkshire County Council, North York Moors National Park Authority, North Yorkshire Moors Railway, Ryedale District Council, Ryedale Folk Museum and The National Trust.

I gratefully acknowledge the permission given by the authors and publishers of the books used for the short quotations throughout this publication. Every effort has been made to trace the copyright holders for these quotations, unfortunately in some instances I have been unable to do so and would therefore be grateful for any information that may assist me in contacting these copyright holders. Full credits to author and title have been given within the text as well as in the comprehensive bibliography at the back of this book.

Front cover photograph 'Old Ralph Cross, Blakey Ridge'
Back cover photograph 'Farndale from Blakey Ridge'
© Julie Fryer, Wigton, Cumbria.

Back cover photograph: 'Birch Hall Inn, Beck Hole' © Mark Reid
8-page colour photographs insert © Mark Reid & Peter Neusser

Illustrations © John A. Ives, Dringhouses, York.
www.johnaives.co.uk

Printed and bound by Spectrum Print, Cleethorpes.

This guidebook was researched, written, typeset, printed and bound in England.

A FOREWORD BY NICHOLAS RHEA

Nicholas Rhea is a pseudonym of Peter N. Walker who has written more than 100 titles, including crime novels and books about the North York Moors. Britain's most popular TV drama, Heartbeat, is based on his 'Constable' series and he is delighted that it is set on the moors – with an inn playing a significant role.

Both sets of my grandparents owned inns on the North York Moors, and I was born and reared at Glaisdale within sight of my grandad Rhea's Angler's Rest, (formerly The Three Blast Furnaces and now The Moon and Sixpence) then I spent most of my working life in and around the area. While growing up, I explored the moors on foot and on my bike, so even if I had not become an author, I reckon I would have been qualified to pen this foreword - but when Mark Reid asked me, I felt quite humbled because his work so beautifully captures the very essence of the moors in a style that has eluded many other writers.

It follows that this is no ordinary guidebook. In addition to its well-researched information, it exudes true emotion along with a genuine understanding and deep love of the countryside through which we are carefully shepherded. Mark leads us with a steady hand, for he has an uncanny knack of making us want to see what is around the next corner or over the next summit - and when that is the welcoming presence of a moorland inn, then our spirits are lifted and our hearts rejoice!

There is nothing new about the role of the country inn. Down the centuries, travellers have sought refuge, refreshment and accommodation within their stout and friendly walls and Mark has revived the ancient skill of completing a journey by travelling from inn to inn, albeit now for leisure purposes rather than from necessity.

That makes it all the more interesting and infinitely more enjoyable - there is the time and opportunity to discover the delights which surround us, whether in the form of history, nature, topography or legend, and Mark has taken the time to check, quite literally, every inch of the way.

To complete this tour is to discover not only the moors and the inns, but also oneself.

Beggar's Bridge

CONTENTS

· ·

Overview Map	5
Foreword by Nicholas Rhea	6
Introduction	9
Plan of the Book	11
Route Descriptions and Rights of Way	13
The Maps	16
Key to the Maps	17
Safety	18
Countryside Code	21
Useful Information	23
Facilities provided at each of the Overnight Stops	26
Public Houses	28
Breweries	36
The History of the North York Moors	42
The Geology of the North York Moors	49
Fauna and Flora of the North York Moors	52
Stage One - *Helmsley to Hutton-le-Hole* (14 miles)	54
Stage Two - *Hutton-le-Hole to Levisham* (13 miles)	82
Stage Three - *Levisham to Egton Bridge* (15 miles)	103
Stage Four - *Egton Bridge to Rosedale Abbey* (15 miles)	131
Stage Five - *Rosedale Abbey to Hawnby* (16 miles)	155
Stage Six - *Hawnby to Helmsley* (16 miles)	180
Bibliography	204
The Inn Way 'Log Book'	217

INTRODUCTION

The North York Moors are a place of solitude and peace, a place where thoughts run deep. The Moors are the preserve of the relative few who take pleasure in walking across England's largest expanse of heather moorland, to marvel at the countless Bronze Age remains, ecclesiastical treasures, gently rolling moors and lush valleys that seem to have been scooped out of the hills. There is so much here, so much contrast and yet a uniformity that pervades its every corner. Perhaps this is due to the people that live here. The people of the Moors and their communities are still thriving and have not succumbed to the worst excesses of tourism. It is these people that add a different dimension to the whole experience of visiting the Moors, their character, traditions and overall way of life whether it be the important yet somehow peculiar Court Leet of the Manor of Spaunton, game of quoits on a village green or a darts match in a local pub played on a 'Yorkshire' board (which differs from the 'standard' dartboard). There is so much more to experience in the North York Moors than can ever be seen through the tinted glass of a car windscreen. It is a place with a very special character all of its own. The only real way to understand this is by walking through it, seeing and feeling it in its every mood and talking to the people of the Moors.

For the past two years I have walked along exhilarating paths across ridges and escarpments, explored countless old tracks across heather moorland and day-dreamed on grassy slopes in the warm afternoon sun, covering over 650 miles of footpaths and scribbling in my notebook as I went. I hope this was the reason for the curious glances from others as I walked through villages and along quiet country lanes. Occasionally, curiosity would get the better of some people and after commenting on the weather would ask me what I was doing up here in the North York Moors on a Tuesday afternoon. They would also ask me why. Not why was I writing a book, but why the North York Moors? Surely there was not enough of interest here to fill a book, as once you have seen one moor you have seen them all, especially that drab stretch of moorland they had to drive across to get to Whitby. What do they want? How inconsiderate of the North York Moors not to present itself in all of its glory for the benefit of the speeding motorist to glance at whilst overtaking a caravan along the A169. Heaven forbid that they actually get out of their car with its climate control system and CD player to have a closer look. But there again, why try and persuade them?

In answer to the question posed in the Introduction to *The Inn Way...to the English Lake District,* nowhere has yet come close to rivalling Swaledale as, in my opinion, the most beautiful valley in the world. On the other hand, ask me again if I'm sat enjoying a pint on a warm summer's evening outside the Horseshoe Hotel at Egton Bridge and I may change my mind. Cheers!

Bransdale Mill

PLAN OF THE BOOK

The Inn Way...to the North York Moors will take six days to complete either as an 89-mile circular walk or broken down into individual linear walks of up to sixteen miles. Each walk has its own section within this book, designed to provide all of the necessary information for that day's walk. These individual sections contain an information page, route description, hand drawn map and a detailed compilation of information concerning places of interest along the way that are brought to life by a selection of fascinating short quotations from selected travel authors who have visited the North York Moors over the last hundred years.

Interpretation of Information and Route Descriptions

Walk Information

Points of interest:	This provides a summary of the highlights of the day's walk.
Distance:	The distance travelled in a day has been broken down into 'morning' and 'afternoon' sections with a total mileage for the day. All distances given are 'map miles' estimated from Ordnance Survey (1:25,000) maps. All distances quoted are in miles and yards, conversions as follows: Yards to metres multiply by 0.9 Miles to kilometres multiply by 1.6 Kilometres to miles multiply by 0.6 Metres to yards multiply by 1.1
Time:	Total time taken to complete the day's walk. This is based upon a walking speed of two-and-a-half miles per hour with consideration for steep ascents, rest stops and viewpoints. This time does not include the obligatory hour lunch break!

Terrain:	Summary of the type of walking surface you will encounter along the way, for example stony tracks, boggy ground etc, as well as any particularly steep ascents or descents and exposed sections.
Ascents:	Each of the major climbs of the day are listed complete with maximum height gained. This figure is not necessarily the total amount of climbing to be done as most ascents start between 100 and 300 metres above sea level. All height figures are in metres (see conversion table above).
Viewpoints:	A selection of the best viewpoints for each section - remember your camera as well as your binoculars!

Facilities

Inn	See list of 'Public Houses'
B&B	Bed and Breakfast accommodation available in the village.
Shop	At least one shop selling general provisions.
PO	Post Office, many of which sell limited provisions.
Café	Teas and light refreshments available.
Bus	Served by public transport, although services are often seasonal and infrequent.
Train	Served by either the Esk Valley Line or the North Yorkshire Moors Railway.
Phone	Public payphone
Toilets	Public conveniences
Info	Tourist Information Centres or National Park Information Centres.
YH	Youth Hostel accommodation available in or near the village.
Camp	Campsite in or near the village.

ROUTE DESCRIPTIONS & RIGHTS OF WAY

. . . .

Route Descriptions

The following abbreviations have been used throughout the route descriptions:

SP	Signpost
FP	Footpath
BW	Bridleway
FB	Footbridge
YH	Youth Hostel
Approx.	Approximately

Route finding in the North York Moors National Park is generally easy as most routes are well marked with signposts and waymarkers. These are often colour-coded as follows: yellow for footpaths, blue for bridleways and red for byways. Often, the path on the ground is clearly defined and easy to follow, however, some sections cross more remote areas and open moorland where route finding may be more difficult with few landmarks and featureless terrain, especially in bad weather. Many moorland paths are marked by a series of small cairns, or heaps of stones, which help to identify the route. *Always take up-to-date OS maps with you as well as a compass or GPS.*

The route has been walked several times using solely the route descriptions given, however, to ensure ease of use they should be used in conjunction with the hand drawn maps that appear within the text, with an OS map as back-up. Each route description has been divided into paragraphs that correspond with one of these detailed hand-drawn maps.

A reasonable walking speed is 3 mph, although this averages out to around 2.5 mph over the course of a day. With this in mind, it will take about 5 minutes to walk 0.25 miles, 10 minutes to walk 0.5 miles and 20 minutes to walk 1 mile.

Grid References

Grid References have been given within the Route Descriptions to assist route finding; for example the Grid Reference for Helmsley Church is SE 612 839 and for Church Bridge near Hawnby is SE 535 899.

Rights of Way

Public Rights of Way or Open Access land must be used during the completion of this walk. On some occasions the path on the ground differs very slightly from the Right of Way shown on the OS map. Where this occurs I have followed the path on the ground to avoid creating more paths and consequently more erosion.

The countryside is slowly but constantly evolving and changing; stiles may become bridle-gates, gates may disappear, paths may be re-surfaced, pubs or shops may close. Footpath repair and conservation work is an important and never ending job within the National Park and occasionally Rights of Way may be altered or diverted to prevent further erosion damage or to simply improve the line of the footpath. Any changes and diversions will be clearly signposted and must be followed, and are usually marked on the most up-to-date Ordnance Survey maps. Feedback concerning these changes is always welcome, as this book is updated at each reprint.

Open Access

The Countryside and Rights of Way Act 2000 opened up 4,000 square miles of mountain, moor, heath, down and common land throughout England. Walkers can now freely roam across this Open Access land without having to stay on public footpaths. These new rights of access relate to mapped areas of access land that comprise predominantly of unenclosed areas of mountains, hills and moorland - not enclosed fields or private land - and are marked on Ordnance Survey maps as areas of yellow shading. On the ground, key access points display a brown circular Open Access symbol as well as local information. Generally, you can get onto Access Land via existing

Rights of Way or moorland roads. Farmers and landowners can restrict access rights to their land for 28 days each year, for example during the breeding season. They may also apply for long term restrictions where necessary for land management, safety or fire prevention. Restrictions or closures are shown on the Countryside Access website or on local notices. Walkers using Open Access land have a responsibility to respect and protect the countryside and follow the Countryside Code.

Long sections of *The Inn Way... to the North York Moors* follow existing Rights of Way across Open Access land, primarily across the high moorland of the central North York Moors. Some sections of this walk also follow paths and tracks across Open Access land that link up existing Rights of Way, most notably above Newton Dale, through Cropton Forest and across the moorland ridge between Bransdale and Bilsdale. Always take your Ordnance Survey maps with you so you can take full advantage of this Open Access land.

For further information visit *www.openaccess.gov.uk*

THE MAPS

. . . .

The hand drawn maps are based upon the Ordnance Survey Outdoor Leisure (1:25,000) series of maps and are designed to tie in with the route descriptions. The route is easy to follow and is marked by a series of dots along footpaths and bridleways or arrows along roads and tracks (see 'Key to Maps'). Landmarks, places of interest, hills and selected contours are also given to help you. These maps should guide you safely around *The Inn Way...to the North York Moors*; however, they do not show the surrounding countryside in detail.

Always take Ordnance Survey Explorer maps (scale 1:25,000) with you on your walk, as well as a compass or GPS

Ordnance Survey Explorer Map OL26 (1:25,000)
'North York Moors Western area'. This map covers Helmsley, Hawnby, Bransdale, Farndale and Hutton-le-Hole.

Ordnance Survey Explorer Map OL27 (1:25,000)
'North York Moors Eastern area'. This map covers Newton Dale, Goathland and Esk Dale.

KEY TO MAPS

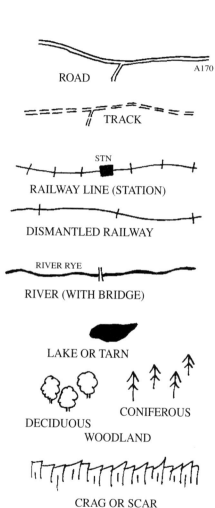

ROAD

TRACK

RAILWAY LINE (STATION)

DISMANTLED RAILWAY

RIVER RYE

RIVER (WITH BRIDGE)

LAKE OR TARN

DECIDUOUS

CONIFEROUS

WOODLAND

CRAG OR SCAR

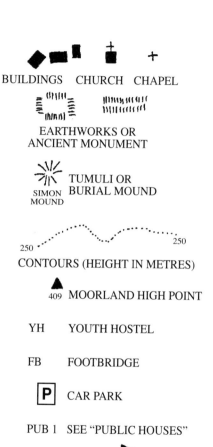

BUILDINGS   CHURCH   CHAPEL

EARTHWORKS OR
ANCIENT MONUMENT

SIMON
MOUND

TUMULI OR
BURIAL MOUND

250   250

CONTOURS (HEIGHT IN METRES)

409 MOORLAND HIGH POINT

YH   YOUTH HOSTEL

FB   FOOTBRIDGE

P   CAR PARK

PUB 1   SEE "PUBLIC HOUSES"

"THE INN WAY" ROUTE
ALONG PATHS/TRACKS/ROADS

SAFETY

· ·

• Never underestimate the strenuous nature of walking particularly when this is combined with high ground and the elements. Do not attempt to complete a walk that is beyond your skill, experience or level of fitness.

• Obtain a detailed weather forecast before setting out on your walk. If the weather turns bad then turn back the way you have walked. Conditions can change for the worse within minutes reducing visibility and making walking hazardous with cloud, mist, strong winds and rain all year round. The temperature, wind speed and general weather conditions on exposed moorland can vary significantly from the conditions in sheltered valleys. The North York Moors, particularly in the eastern area, are prone to a thick, damp sea fog, known locally as a 'roak', which rolls in from the coast across the moors reducing visibility and temperature considerably.

• Take Ordnance Survey maps (1:25,000) of the area. It is essential to carry a compass or GPS (Global Positioning System) as there is mile upon mile of expansive heather moorland at the heart of the North York Moors. This moorland has very few landmarks making it easy to get lost, especially in cloud or fog.

• Your boots are the most important thing; make sure that they are waterproof, comfortable and have good ankle support and sturdy soles. The wrong footwear can mean every step is blisteringly painful - and you will make over 26,000 strides on a 12-mile walk!

• It is important to wear a 'layering system' of clothing as follows: base layer to wick moisture away (long-sleeved T-shirt), insulating mid layer (fleece) and a waterproof and breathable outer shell (waterproof coat and over-trousers), plus walking trousers and a suitable hat and pair of gloves. Gaiters are useful to protect your lower legs when walking through heather or bracken. Wear clothing that is made from synthetic fibres, which are quick drying and help 'wick' moisture away from your skin. Avoid cotton and jeans as these soak up moisture.

- Travel light as a heavy rucksack can tire you out, cause backache and make your shoulders sore. Take essential items such as a spare fleece, nourishing snack food, basic first aid kit, blister plasters, hat, sun cream, whistle, water bottle (minimum 1 litre), torch (and spare batteries), watch, 'survival' bag and mobile 'phone. Line your rucksack with a large plastic bag to keep the contents dry.

- Drink plenty of fluids (not alcohol) and eat food regularly to keep energy levels up. Always take lunch with you as well as high energy snack foods. Carry more food than you think you will need.

- Regularly check your location against the map and route description. Always look for at least three landmarks to confirm your location. If you become misplaced (or lost), re-trace your steps back to your last known location.

- Always walk in a group unless you are very experienced and inform someone of your intended route and report your safe arrival. If you are delayed but safe then make sure you let someone know so that the Mountain Rescue Team is not called out.

- Mobile phone coverage in the North York Moors is patchy due to the nature of the landscape, with reception limited to the high moors as well as the larger villages and towns such as Helmsley. Many of the more remote valleys have no reception at all. In an emergency, go to the nearest village or farmhouse to use a phone.

- In an emergency in a remote and inaccessible location call out the Mountain Rescue Team by 'phoning 999 and asking for Mountain Rescue (via the Police), giving details of the incident and location. If you do not have a mobile 'phone then summon help with six blasts of your whistle or flashes of your torch. *NB: Mountain Rescue is an Emergency Service*

- Take care when crossing rivers, roads or railway lines and walk in single file (facing oncoming traffic) when walking along country lanes. Do not explore old mine or quarry workings. Never attempt to cross flooded land or a stream/river that is in flood.

• Keep dogs under close control, preferably on a lead. Dogs and livestock can be dangerous, particularly cows with calves. If you come across cows with their calves whilst walking your dog, do not walk between them but walk around them giving them a wide berth. If a situation appears to be developing, look for a way of leaving the enclosure safely. If you feel threatened let the dog go as it can run faster than a cow, and this will make you less of a threat. Once you have let your dog go, leave the enclosure then recall your dog when it is safe to do so.

• The North York Moors are home to Britain's only poisonous snake, the Adder. Adders like south-facing slopes and can often be found basking in the sun. Adders will only bite if they are startled or scared - if you are unlucky enough to be bitten seek medical help immediately.

• Above all, keep your hands out of your pockets and look where you are going!

REMEMBER: *"An experienced walker knows when to turn back"*

Rievaulx

COUNTRYSIDE CODE

Consider other people

Showing consideration and respect for other people makes the countryside a pleasant environment for everyone – at home, at work and at leisure.

Enjoy the countryside and respect its life and work

Do not touch crops, machinery or livestock. We have a responsibility to protect our countryside now and for future generations, so make sure you don't harm animals, birds, plants or trees. Wild animals and farm animals can behave unpredictably if you get too close, especially if they're with their young – so give them plenty of space.

Tread gently – discover the beauty of the natural environment and take care not to damage, destroy or remove features such as rocks, plants and trees. They provide homes and food for wildlife, and add to everybody's enjoyment of the countryside.

Leave gates and property as you find them

Please respect the working life of the countryside, as our actions can affect people's livelihoods, our heritage, and the safety and welfare of animals and ourselves. Use stiles and gates to cross fences and walls and close gates behind you. When walking across fields with crops follow the paths wherever possible. Our heritage belongs to all of us – be careful not to disturb ruins and historic sites.

Keep to public Rights of Way or Open Access areas.

Footpaths are for walkers; bridleways are for cyclists, horse-riders and walkers. Motorbikes and cars should keep to roads.

Do not make excessive noise

The moors and valleys should be quiet places

Take care on country roads

Face oncoming traffic and walk in single file

Safeguard water supplies

Moorland streams are used by livestock and often feed reservoirs for drinking supplies. Do not foul water supplies.

Guard against risk of fire
Uncontrolled fires can devastate moorland, which may never fully recover.
Do not start fires or drop matches.

Keep dogs under control
A loose dog can be catastrophic for ground nesting birds, sheep and
sometimes the dog itself. Your dog must be under control so that it does
not disturb or scare farm animals or wildlife. By law, farmers are entitled
to destroy a dog that injures or worries their animals. If a farm animal
chases you and your dog, it is safer to let your dog off the lead – don't risk
getting hurt by trying to protect it. Clear up after your dog and make
sure your dog is wormed regularly.

Take litter home
Litter is dangerous and unsightly.

Safety
Weather can change quickly, are you fully equipped for the hills?
You're responsible for your own safety and for others in your care, so be
prepared for the unexpected; follow local advice and signs. Use up-to-date
OS maps. Part of the appeal of the countryside is that you can get away
from it all. You may not see anyone for hours and there are many places
without mobile-phone signals, so let someone know where you're
going and when you expect to return.

USEFUL INFORMATION

If you are travelling by public transport make sure that you check train and bus times before you set out as these often vary seasonally. Book accommodation in advance as B&Bs and Youth Hostels can get fully booked up during the summer months and may close temporarily during the winter months.

InnWay Publications Website: www.innway.co.uk
A comprehensive site with detailed information to help organise your walk.

North York Moors National Park Visitor Centres:
Sutton Bank Information Centre: 01845 597426
The Moors Centre, Danby, Esk Dale: 01439 772737
Old Coastguard Station, Robin Hood's Bay: 01947 885900
National Park Centres offer in-depth local knowledge as well as fascinating interpretative displays of the history of the North York Moors, issues facing the area and an insight into life on the Moors in general through various forms of media. They also form a contact point for the Ranger Service and weather information.

Tourist Information Centres (TIC):
Helmsley: 01439 770173
Pickering: 01751 473791
Thirsk: 01845 522755
Whitby: 01723 383637

Public Transport:
Traveline (including Moorsbus): 0871 200 22 33
A 'one stop' information line for national, regional and local bus and train services. Moorsbus operate a Sunday and Bank Holiday service from April until October, with daily services during the main summer holidays to most villages and tourist attractions in the National Park.
Website: www.traveline.org.uk

National Express bookings: 08717 818181
North Yorkshire Moors Railway: 01751 472508
Rail enquiries: 08457 484950
The nearest railway station to Helmsley is at Thirsk.

Baggage Courier Service:
Brigantes Baggage Courier: 01729 830463
Rookery Cottage
Kirkby Malham
Skipton
North Yorkshire, BD23 4BX
Website: www.brigantesenglishwalks.com

Organisations:
North York Moors National Park Authority: 01439 770657
The Old Vicarage
Bondgate
Helmsley, North Yorkshire
Website: www.northyorkmoors-npa.gov.uk

Welcome to Yorkshire 0113 322 3500
Dry Sand Foundry
Foundry Square, Leeds
Website: www.yorkshire.com

Yorkshire Moors and Coast Tourism 01845 523877
49b Market Place
Thirsk, North Yorkshire
Website: www.yorkshiremoorsandcoast.com

Youth Hostel Association: 01629 592700
Trevelyan House
Dimple Road
Matlock
Derbyshire
Youth Hostels are located at Helmsley and Lockton (near Levisham).
Website: www.yha.org.uk

Rambler's Association: 020 7339 8500
2nd Floor, Camelford House
87-90 Albert Embankment
London, SE1 7TW
Website: www.ramblers.org.uk

Campaign for Real Ale CAMRA: 01727 867201
230 Hatfield Road
St Albans
Hertfordshire
Website: www.camra.org.uk

Dalby Forest (Forestry Commission):   01751 460295
Dalby Forest Visitor Centre
Low Dalby
Pickering
Website: www.forestry.gov.uk

North Yorkshire County Council: 01609 780780
County Hall
Northallerton
North Yorkshire
Website: www.northyorks.gov.uk

Weather Information
MetOffice Weathercall   09014 722 067
Information supplied by Met Office. Premium Rate calls.
Website: www.metoffice.gov.uk

For a detailed accommodation guide send a
Stamped Addressed Envelope to:
InnWay Publications, 102 Leeds Road, Harrogate HG2 8HB.

FACILITIES PROVIDED AT EACH OF THE OVERNIGHT STOPS

··

Stage One - Helmsley

Helmsley serves as the starting and finishing point because it is easy to get to and has plenty of facilities. It is an attractive small town set on the south-western edge of the North York Moors, a popular tourist destination due to its attractive market place, interesting shops, historic church and magnificent castle ruins.

How to get there:

By public transport - the nearest train station is at Thirsk, or why not arrive in style aboard a steam train along the North Yorkshire Moors Railway between Grosmont (connections with the Esk Valley Line) and Pickering. There are frequent bus services connecting Helmsley with Northallerton, Thirsk, York, Malton, Pickering, Scarborough and Hull. The Moorsbus provides frequent services to and from surrounding towns and cities as well as a comprehensive service throughout the North York Moors during the summer months.

By car - Helmsley lies on the A170 between Thirsk and Scarborough at the junction with the B1257 from the North East via Bilsdale, which joins the A170 in the Market Place. There is limited long stay parking available at Helmsley, so please make use of the public transport network and save time, money, hassle and the environment!

Facilities - Helmsley is a busy small market town with a good selection of shops, facilities and amenities aimed at both locals and visitors with a bustling market day on Friday. Facilities include Barclays, NatWest and HSBC banks, a well-stocked Tourist Information Centre (Helmsley Castle), outdoor pursuits shops, small supermarket, general stores, hardware shop, newsagent, bakery, delicatessen, sandwich shop, gift shops, bookshop, Post Office, cafés, garage, doctors' surgery, fish & chip shop, restaurants, Police station, telephones, toilets, Youth Hostel, car park (limited long stay), Arts

Centre, North York Moors National Park Authority offices and a good selection of hotels, pubs and bed and breakfasts.

Stage Two - Hutton-le-Hole

Hutton-le-Hole offers bed and breakfast accommodation, a hotel, caravan site, bus service, car park, telephone, toilets, National Park Information Point, Ryedale Folk Museum, cafés, gift shops, village shop and the Crown Inn.

Stage Three - Levisham

Levisham offers bed and breakfast accommodation, country house hotel, telephone, train station, café (train station), toilets (train station), and the Horseshoe Inn.

Stage Four - Egton Bridge

Egton Bridge offers bed and breakfast accommodation, restaurant, train station (Esk Valley Line), car park, toilets, telephone, the Postgate Inn and the Horseshoe Hotel. *(Egton 'on the hill' is a brisk 15-minute walk away up a steep hill and offers B&Bs and two pubs).*

Stage Five - Rosedale Abbey

Rosedale Abbey offers a selection of bed and breakfasts, large campsite, bus service, car parks, toilets, telephone, tea rooms, general stores, farm shop, glass workshop, 9-hole golf course and three pubs. *Please Note: There are no B&Bs in the heart of the village of Rosedale Abbey itself, although several can be found within a mile radius.*

Stage Six - Hawnby

Hawnby offers bed and breakfast accommodation, telephone, shop, tearooms and the Inn at Hawnby.

All of the above information is for guide purposes only and many facilities are liable to change. If it is important – check it.

PUBLIC HOUSES

The route of *The Inn Way...to the North York Moors* is designed to take in as many of the area's 'classic' country pubs as possible. I am sure you will agree that the thirty-one pubs detailed below are amongst the finest you will find anywhere for their warmth, character and charm. All pubs encountered along the route have been listed - I'll let you make up your own mind as to your favourite ones. NB: If you are relying on a pub for lunchtime food then it is advisable to 'phone in advance to check opening times.

1.   *The Feathers, Helmsley: 01439 770275*

The Pickwick Bar is situated to the side of the Feathers Hotel, an elegant three storey Georgian house that was the local doctors' house for generations. Originally known as Thorpe's Cottage, this 15th Century building has a great deal of character with oak beams, open fires, 'Mousey' Thompson furniture and a stone-flagged floor.
ACC / FOOD / FIRE / GDN / TRAD / BAR

2.   *Black Swan, Helmsley: 01439 770466*

This historic coaching inn incorporates three buildings of considerable age with the Georgian and Tudor architecture clearly visible, which combine together to form a very attractive building indeed; the black and white house was once the vicarage. In the coaching days a regular service ran from this inn to London. Several well appointed lounges offer refreshments in comfortable surroundings with wood panelling and open fires. There is also an adjoining tea rooms.
ACC / FOOD / FIRE / GDN / TRAD

3.   *Crown Inn, Helmsley: 01439 770297*

This 16th Century coaching inn has lots of different rooms including a cosy public bar and a comfortable lounge with wood panelling as well as open fires.
ACC / FOOD / FIRE / GDN / TRAD

4.   Royal Oak, Helmsley: 01439 770450

This traditional pub dates back to 1861 and overlooks the Market Place, its colourful hanging baskets and window boxes a delight in summer. A central bar serves three drinking areas of lounge, games area and bar complete with wooden floorboards and an open fire. With an emphasis on live music, entertainment and sport, the Oak boasts a lively atmosphere in the evenings.

ACC / FOOD / FIRE / GDN / TRAD / BAR

5.   Feversham Arms Hotel, Church Street, Helmsley: 01439 770766

This luxurious multi award-winning hotel dates back to 1855 when the original Bay Horse Inn was destroyed by fire and this 'new' inn was built by the Earl of Feversham. Inside, the hotel blends traditional with contemporary in a stylish way with a comfortable lounge bar at the front of the hotel. Works of art adorn the walls, whilst adjoining the hotel is a spa, pool and terrace complex.

ACC / FOOD / FIRE / GDN / TRAD

6.   Star Inn, Harome: 01439 770397

Beautiful cruck-framed thatched cottage of immense character and charm with low beams, flagged floor, candle-lit corners, open fires and carefully arranged bric-a-brac. This inn dates back to the 14th Century and is said to have originally been built as a monastic hostelry on the road between Whitby and York. A separate restaurant and upstairs 'coffee loft' add space to an otherwise cosy bar whose dark oak tables, chairs and bar counter were crafted by 'Mousey' Thompson of Kilburn. Always busy with people who come to savour the award-winning food.

ACC / FOOD / FIRE / GDN / TRAD / BAR / INN

Addendum - Pheasant Hotel, Harome: 01439 771241

This comfortable hotel boasts fine views across the village pond from its extensive sun terrace and gardens. Inside, there is a small bar with flagstone floor warmed by a large fireplace.

ACC / FOOD / FIRE / GDN

7. Plough Inn, Wombleton: 01751 431356

This very appealing traditional village local lies in the heart of the quiet village of Wombleton. The comfortable interior is warmed by open fires, which add to the welcome. A separate dining area is housed in a 15th Century cruck-framed cottage of considerable character.

FOOD / FIRE / GDN / TRAD

8. Plough Inn, Fadmoor: 01751 431515

Tucked away off the village green, the Plough Inn is a very comfortable yet traditional village local with an 'olde worlde' bar area warmed by a cast iron range, wonderfully cosy 'snug' complete with its own fireplace, separate dining area, small coffee lounge and lots of nooks and crannies.

FOOD / FIRE / GDN / TRAD / BAR / INN

9. Royal Oak Inn, Gillamoor: 01751 431414

This traditional country inn has an unrivalled location facing onto the narrow village green. The interior of this Grade II listed inn retains a great deal of character with oak beams and open fires.

ACC / FOOD / FIRE / GDN / TRAD / INN

10. Crown, Hutton-le-Hole: 01751 417343

Set in the heart of the picture-postcard village of Hutton-le-Hole, this popular village pub has been run by the same family for over 40 years. During the 19th Century many miners from the Rosedale ironstone mines lived at Hutton where they slaked their thirsts; the Crown was once the village smithy shop but became an inn two hundred years ago. Note the impressive collection of jugs hanging from the ceiling.

FOOD / FIRE / GDN / TRAD

11. Blacksmiths Arms, Lastingham: 01751 417247

Unspoilt 17th Century country pub in the heart of the village overlooking the historic church. A pub of great character that has retained its original layout including a small bar complete with cast iron range, separate dining room, snug and back bar as well as a sheltered beer garden.

ACC / FOOD / FIRE / GDN / TRAD / BAR / INN

12. New Inn, Cropton: 01751 417330

The New Inn serves as the 'brewery tap' for the Cropton Brewery, which is situated behind the pub, and as such always has a superb range of Real Ales on offer. The pub boasts a comfortable lounge, games room, family room, restaurant and extensive beer garden where you can sample a pint or two of their award-winning ales, or why not go on a brewery tour?
ACC / FOOD / GDN / TRAD

13. White Swan, Newton-on-Rawcliffe: 01751 472505

Situated in the heart of the quiet village of Newton, the White Swan looks out across the village green complete with duck pond. The cosy bar of this traditional country pub is warmed by a log fire. Campsite attached to the pub. Limited lunchtime opening.
FOOD / FIRE / GDN / TRAD / BAR

14. Horseshoe Inn, Levisham: 01751 460240

Standing proudly at the top of the long village green, this former farmhouse dates back to the 16th Century. The comfortable opened-out interior retains a great deal of charm with dark wood floorboards and a lovely stone fireplace, whilst the extensive beer garden to the front of the pub even boasts a maypole!
ACC / FOOD / FIRE / GDN / TRAD

15. Spout Bar, Mallyan Spout Hotel, Goathland: 01947 896486

The Spout Bar lies to the side of the Mallyan Spout Hotel, an imposing ivy-clad Victorian hotel. This bar boasts wooden floors, cosy corners and a log burning stove. A well-worn footpath leads from the side of the hotel down into the valley of West Beck and the famous Mallyan Spout waterfall.
ACC / FOOD / FIRE / GDN / TRAD / BAR

16. Goathland Hotel, Goathland: 01947 896203

The Goathland Hotel will be instantly recognisable to millions as The Aidensfield Arms, although many still need to ask the bar staff for confirmation. This traditional pub boasts a large bar complete with tiled floor and open fire as well as a separate smaller lounge. The walls

of the bar are adorned with interesting bric-a-brac including the swords of the local Plough Stots team.
ACC / FOOD / FIRE / GDN / TRAD / BAR

17. *Inn on the Moor, Goathland: 01947 896296*
A small wood panelled public bar lies to the side of this large hotel, which caters for the overwhelming number of visitors to this moorland village during the summer. The Inn on the Moor often acted as the 'base camp' for the TV crews when filming 'Heartbeat'.
ACC / FOOD / FIRE / GDN / TRAD

18. *Birch Hall Inn, Beck Hole: 01947 896245*
The bar of this wonderful old pub has a strong claim to the title 'Smallest Bar in the World' - more than four customers and it's heaving! A (slightly) larger lounge and beer garden provide more space whilst sandwiched between the bar and lounge is a tiny shop. This pub remains completely unaltered (The Good Pub Guide 2003 'Unspoilt Pub of the Year') and stands as one of the classic country inns of England.
FOOD / FIRE / GDN / TRAD / BAR / INN

19. *Horseshoe Hotel, Egton Bridge: 01947 895245*
This old inn dates back to the 18th Century and has an idyllic location amongst lawns and mature trees beside the River Esk, with stepping stones leading from beside the pub across the river; exciting to say the least especially after heavy rain! The bar retains a great deal of character with wooden settles and an open fire.
ACC / FOOD / FIRE / GDN / TRAD / BAR / INN

20. *Postgate Inn, Egton Bridge: 01947 895241*
Formerly the Station Hotel, this stone pub dates from when the Esk Valley Railway was opened between Grosmont and Middlesbrough in 1865. The pub was later renamed in honour of Father Postgate, the famous local Catholic martyr. This very comfortable old-fashioned inn was often featured in the TV series Heartbeat when it changed its name again, this time to the Black Dog Inn.
ACC / FOOD / FIRE / GDN / TRAD / BAR

21.   Arncliffe Arms, Glaisdale: 01947 897555

Situated at the end of a row of stone cottages, this traditional pub features a large lounge, bistro, games room and bar with exposed stonework and wood burning stoves where walkers can enjoy a pint next to a warming fire. Glaisdale lies on Wainwright's Coast to Coast walk.

ACC / FOOD / FIRE / GDN / TRAD

22.   The Moon and Sixpence, Glaisdale: CLOSED 2003

This old pub was formerly known as The Three Blast Furnaces in recognition of the ironstone mining industry that once flourished in and around Glaisdale during the 19th Century. The pub then changed its name to the Angler's Rest and, more recently, to the Moon and Sixpence, although it is often referred to as the 'Middle House' locally.

23.   The Mitre Tavern, Glaisdale: CLOSED 2005

Known locally as the 'Top House', the Mitre Tavern enjoys superb views across Esk Dale from its elevated position in the main part of Glaisdale village.

24.   Board Inn, Lealholm: 01947 897279

Lovely location overlooking the village green and beside the graceful stone bridge across the River Esk - a scene of beauty for you to enjoy whilst drinking a well-earned pint from the riverside patio! Inside there is a traditional bar with a stone fireplace and wood-burning stove as well as a separate lounge bar and restaurant with river views. A classic English country inn.

ACC / FOOD / FIRE / GDN / TRAD / BAR / INN

25.   Milburn Arms Hotel, Rosedale Abbey: 01751 417312

This fine stone-built hotel dates back to the 15th Century when it was the Steward's House for the adjacent Priory; it is said that a secret tunnel links the hotel with the Priory. The present building dates from 1776 and retains a great deal of character with low beams, open fires and a small 'snug'.

ACC / FOOD / FIRE / GDN / TRAD

At the time of writing (March 2010) this pub had closed; however, it may re-open in the future.

26. White Horse Farm Inn, Rosedale Abbey: 01751 417239

Situated at the foot of the steep Chimney Bank, this lovely old inn boasts superb views across Rosedale from its beer garden. The pub gained its beer licence in 1702 and continued as a farm and alehouse for many years. When the local ironstone mines were at full production during the 19th Century the inn was used as a lodging house for miners; it is said that the beds never went cold as when one miner got up for his shift another would then jump in for some sleep.
ACC / FOOD / FIRE / GDN / TRAD / BAR

27. Coach House Inn, Rosedale Abbey: 01751 417208

This warm and welcoming pub lies at the heart of the village and is popular with visitors from the nearby caravan and camping site. Divided into three rooms, there is a dining room, comfortable bar complete with wood-burning stove and a games room with pool table.
FOOD / FIRE / GDN / TRAD

28. Feversham Arms, Church Houses: 01751 433206

It comes as quite a surprise to find this lovely old country pub in such a tiny hamlet. The small central bar retains a great deal of character with a stone flagged floor and cast iron range. The Feversham Arms is the only pub in Farndale and perhaps the most remote in the North York Moors. Very popular with walkers, especially in spring when the famous wild daffodils are in bloom.
ACC / FOOD / FIRE / GDN / TRAD / BAR / INN

29. Sun Inn, Bilsdale: 01439 798206

The Sun Inn was built in 1914 as a replacement for the Old Sun Inn, or Spout House, which still stands next door. This 16th Century thatched cruck-framed cottage became a licensed pub in 1714 and remains completely unaltered offering an insight into how country inns used to be. The 'new' Sun Inn is an unpretentious country pub that proudly continues the long tradition of hospitality. For several successive generations the landlord of the Sun Inn has been a William Ainsley; the current William Ainsley is a farmer as well as an innkeeper.
FIRE / GDN / TRAD / BAR / INN

30. Inn at Hawnby, Hawnby: 01439 798202

Beautiful location in 'upper' Hawnby with wonderful views across Ryedale. This inn dates back to at least the early 19th Century, when it was originally known as the Tamworth Arms, and forms part of Lord Mexborough's estate. Comfortable bar with an open fire and a relaxed 'country' atmosphere. Popular with locals, country sports enthusiasts and walkers alike.

ACC / FOOD / FIRE / GDN / TRAD / BAR / INN

31. Hare Inn, Scawton: 01845 597524

Historic country inn of great character with lots of nooks and crannies, interesting bric-a-brac, flagged floor, open fires and an emphasis on food. There has been an inn / farmhouse on this site since at least the 16th Century although the monks of either Rievaulx or Old Byland reputedly established an alehouse here in the 12th Century to refresh the many travellers who passed this way.

FOOD / FIRE / GDN / TRAD / BAR / INN

KEY
. . . .

ACC	Accommodation
FOOD	Substantial snacks or meals available lunchtime and evening
FIRE	Open fires
GDN	Beer garden (includes lawns, patios and outside benches)
TRAD	Cask ales available (Real Ale)
BAR	Traditional public bar area often with stone or wooden floor
INN	Classic country inn

THE BREWERIES

This corner of Yorkshire was once the heartland for two major regional breweries: Camerons and Vaux; sadly Vaux are no more, but Camerons prospers once again. The recent resurgence of small-scale brewing adds interest away from the ubiquitous national brands, and old brewery memorabilia of long forgotten names such as Rose's, Russell & Wrangham and, more recently, Vaux still grace the walls of many inns adding a touch of nostalgic colour. With this in mind, I have only listed independent local or regional breweries whose beers reflect the region in which they are sold, rather than national or international brewers who often concentrate on brand image and profit at the expense of regional identity.

Most pubs within the North York Moors National Park are free houses, with a handful of tenanted and managed houses in the larger villages and towns. This means that the licensees are free to choose whichever brand he or she likes; however, in reality trade deals and discounts often dictate which products an outlet sells, although the now common 'guest beer' adds variety, all of which means that you may find a whole range of beers on sale that are not listed below.

INDEPENDENT REGIONAL BREWERS
Black Sheep Brewery
Wellgarth, Masham, North Yorkshire

This independent brewery was set up in 1992 by Paul Theakston following the take-over in 1987 of his old family firm by Scottish and Newcastle Breweries, as they were then known. The brewery is situated in the former Lightfoot Brewery maltings literally next door to the old offices of T&R Theakston Ltd; Lightfoot's were Masham's 'other' brewery, purchased by Theakston's in 1919. Black Sheep Brewery produces a range of traditional Yorkshire 'style' beers using only the finest ingredients and traditional brewing plant rescued from Hartley's of Ulverston. The pronounced bitterness and characteristic flavour of the beers is reminiscent of some of the old West Riding brews, mainly due to the fact that traditional Yorkshire Square fermenting vessels are used. In spring 2004, a second brew-house was installed to run in parallel with their existing brew-house, which has almost doubled capacity to around 80,000 barrels a year. Black Sheep Brewery only supply to the free trade on a rapidly increasing geographical basis. Black Sheep Ale is a superb example of a Yorkshire strong ale and well worth sampling if you come across it. *Cask ales available include Best Bitter (ABV 3.8%), Golden Sheep (ABV 3.9%), Black Sheep Ale (ABV 4.4%) and Riggwelter (ABV 5.9%).*

Camerons Brewery Ltd.
Lion Brewery, Hartlepool.

With a heritage that dates back to 1865, this once famous Teesside brewery went through a period of change during the 1970s and 80s and was threatened with closure until Wolverhampton & Dudley Breweries took control of the brewery along with a small estate of 51 pubs in 1992; the bulk of the former Camerons tied estate went to form the Pubmaster pub company. W&DB invested heavily in Camerons Brewery, its pubs and its Strongarm brand, known locally as Ruby Red, which was originally brewed to slake the thirsts of the men of industrial Teesside. In 2002 the owners of Castle Eden Brewery purchased the Lion Brewery from W&DB to safeguard the future of brewing at Hartlepool, with the subsequent closure of their Castle Eden site. Camerons is now a totally independent regional brewing company, the last remaining in the North East, with an expanding estate of around 150 tied houses and extensive free trade. Camerons bought Russell & Wrangham of Malton in 1961 which provided many outlets in the Vale of Pickering and southern moors. *Cask ales available include Camerons Best Bitter (ABV 3.6%), Strongarm (ABV 4%), Trophy Special (ABV 4%), plus a range of seasonal ales.*

Captain Cook Brewery
The White Swan, Stokesley, North Yorkshire.

This small micro-brewery is located in an out-building behind The White Swan in the delightful old Yorkshire market town of Stokesley. The brewery was opened in 1999 by James Cook, a regular of the White Swan! *Cask ales available include Sunset (ABV 4.0%), Slipway (ABV 4.2%), Midships (ABV 4.1%), Black Porter (ABV 4.4%).*

Cropton Brewery

Woolcroft, The New Inn, Cropton, North Yorkshire.

The Cropton Brewery first began brewing in the cellars of the New Inn in 1984 because, according to local folklore, many people in the village feared that beer supplies might be disrupted during the harsh winter months - the obvious answer was for the pub to brew their own! Such was the success of this venture that by 1994 the brewery relocated to a purpose-built brewery behind the pub. Their extensive range of award-winning ales, many of them powerful brews at over 4.0% ABV, can be sampled at the New Inn, its 'brewery tap', or why not go on a tour of the brewery? Monkman's Slaughter won the Gold Medal in the Strong Bitters Category of the Champion Beer of Britain competition at the CAMRA Great British Beer Festival 2000, adding to a clutch of other awards. *Cask ales available include Two Pints (ABV 4.0%), Honey Gold Bitter (ABV 4.2%), Scoresby Stout (ABV 4.2%), Yorkshire Moors (ABV 4.6%), Monkman's Slaughter (ABV 6.0%), plus seasonal ales.*

Daleside Brewery

Starbeck, Harrogate, North Yorkshire.

This Harrogate brewery, originally called Big End, mashed its first brew in 1987 and now supplies a large and far-flung free trade market with its extensive range of award-winning ales, some of which are rather unusual. Morocco Ale (bottled) is a highly spiced beer which uses ginger in the brewing process, the inspiration for which came from an old 17th Century recipe from Levens Hall in Cumbria. Crack Shot (bottled) is again based on a 17th Century 'strong winter ale' recipe that was discovered amongst the pages of a 400-year-old cookbook at Ripley Castle. Award-winning Monkey Wrench is well worth sampling to savour its smooth, well-balanced yet complex flavour; this beer won the Strong Ale category in both 1997 and 1998 at the CAMRA Champion Winter Beer of Britain competition. *Cask ales available include Bitter (ABV 3.7%), Blonde (ABV 3.9%), Pride of England (ABV 4.0%), Special Bitter (ABV 4.1%), Old Leg Over (ABV 4.1%), Greengrass Old Rogue Ale (ABV 4.5%), Monkey Wrench (ABV 5.3%) and St George's Ale (ABV 5.3%)*

The Durham Brewery

Unit 5A, Bowburn North Industrial Estate, Bowburn, Co. Durham.

The Durham Brewery was established in 1994 by Steve and Christine Gibbs, who both gave up careers as music teachers in favour of brewing! Situated a few miles from the historic city of Durham, this brewery has gone from strength to strength and now produces thirty barrels a week for free trade accounts throughout County Durham, Yorkshire and the North East. They produce a huge array of award-winning ales including their 'white' range of beers, which are quite similar in appearance to lager but (unlike lager) are packed full of flavour due to the use of a wide variety of hops from around the world for each particular brew. *Cask ales available include Magus (ABV 3.8%), White Gold (ABV 4.0%), White Amarillo (ABV 4.1%), White Velvet (ABV 4.2%) plus many more 'rotating' ales including a range of 'dark' and 'gold' beers.*

Hambleton Ales

Melmerby, Ripon, North Yorkshire.

Small brewery established in 1991 in the village of Holme-on-Swale in the Hambleton District of Yorkshire by Nick Stafford, brother of the owner of Dent Brewery in Cumbria. The name of the company, beers and white horse logo were inspired by the famous White Horse of Kilburn, a huge landscape figure on the flanks of the Hambleton Hills which rise up from the flat Vale of York. Hambleton produces four varieties of bitter ale, which are refreshing and flavoursome. Hambleton Ales have won several CAMRA awards including the Champion Winter Beer of Britain in 1997; of particular note is Stallion, an excellent strong Yorkshire ale. To cope with demand a new brewery was built in 2007 in the village of Melmerby. *Cask ales available include Best Bitter (ABV 3.8%), Stallion (ABV 4.2%), Stud (ABV 4.3%), Nightmare Stout (ABV 5.0%).*

North Yorkshire Brewing Company

Pinchinthorpe Hall, Guisborough.

Based at the historic 17th Century Pinchinthorpe Hall near Guisborough (now a country house hotel and restaurant), the North

Yorkshire Brewing Company produces a huge range of organic beers using natural spring water, all of which can be sampled in the adjoining restaurant or in one of its many free trade accounts. The beer portfolio is impressive ranging from Prior's Ale, a refreshing hoppy bitter, to Rocket Fuel, a strong golden ale. *Cask ales available include Best Bitter (ABV 3.6%), Prior's Ale (ABV 3.6%), Boro Best (ABV 4.0%), Ruby Ale (ABV 4.0%), Cereal Killer (ABV 4.5%), Fools Gold (ABV 4.6%), Flying Herbert (4.7%), Lord Lee's (ABV 4.7%), Rocket Fuel (ABV 5.0%), plus many other ales including seasonal beers.*

T & R Theakston Ltd
Wellgarth, Masham, North Yorkshire.

Established in 1827 in the small Dales town of Masham, this brewery became part of Scottish and Newcastle Breweries, as they were then known, back in 1987. Theakston's ales were then promoted on a national basis, so much so that this once small country brewer became a household name synonymous with Real Ale, indeed, to cope with demand much of the production took place at Scottish Courage's Tyne Brewery. Rather surprisingly, the small Masham brewery remained open producing a limited amount of beer, with a great deal of emphasis placed upon the 'traditional' qualities of the Theakston's brand with its working cooper's shop and picturesque stone-built brewery. Even more surprisingly, the Masham brewery and the Theakston beer brands were sold back to members of the Theakston family in autumn 2003, making this famous and highly regarded traditional brewer once again an independent family-run business. Their most famous brand is the award-winning Theakston's Old Peculier, a legendary strong Yorkshire ale packed full of flavour - drink it with respect! *Cask ales available include Mild (ABV 3.6%), Best Bitter (ABV 3.6%), Black Bull Bitter (ABV 3.9%), XB (ABV 4.6%), Old Peculier (ABV 5.7%), as well as a range of seasonal ales.*

Timothy Taylor & Co.
Knowle Spring Brewery, Keighley, West Yorkshire.

This famous independent Yorkshire brewery dates back to 1858 when Timothy Taylor began brewing in Cook Lane, Keighley. Demand for his quality ales was so great that in 1863 he moved to the

Knowle Spring Brewery, which is still their home. A commitment to producing quality ales using the finest ingredients coupled with traditional brewing methods has paid dividends; indeed they still use Pennine spring water drawn from their own well as the 'liquor' for their award-winning ales. Landlord Pale Ale has won more awards nationally than any other beer and was judged to be the CAMRA Supreme Champion Beer of Britain in 1999 for a record third time. Taylor's brews are characterised by a pronounced bitterness with a distinctive almost floral 'hoppy' taste - the 'Taylor's Taste'. They also brew Golden Best, the last of the Pennine light milds. *Cask ales available include Dark Mild (ABV 3.5%), Golden Best (ABV 3.5%), Porter (ABV 3.8%), Best Bitter (ABV 4%), Landlord (ABV 4.3%), Ram Tam (ABV 4.3%).*

Star Inn, Harome

THE HISTORY OF
THE NORTH YORK MOORS

Millions of us visit this corner of Yorkshire every year to take in the beautiful landscape that makes the North York Moors so special; the rolling heather moorland and gentle meandering valleys cloaked in primeval oak forest. A natural landscape that has changed little over the centuries with a way of life unaltered since people first settled in this region. But this perception is far from the truth. The landscape we see today is the result of over 4,000 years of intervention by man who has modified, shaped and moulded the countryside to suit his needs, a process which continues today. Armed with a little knowledge it is possible to interpret this landscape and look through the ages to discover the legacy of the numerous waves of settlers and invaders whose influence on the landscape has fused together over the centuries to form what we see today.

As temperatures rose after the last Ice Age over 8,000 years ago, the first Stone Age hunter-gatherers began to roam this area, however about 4,000 years ago their primitive stone tools were replaced by more durable metal ones which heralded the onset of the Bronze Age. It was these Bronze Age farmers who first began to manage and control their environment. They lived in somewhat dispersed farming communities, grew crops, raised animals and began to clear the forest that once covered the entire area. The remains of these Bronze Age people can be found in abundance throughout the North York Moors including burial mounds, known locally as 'howes', cairnfields, stone circles, dikes and simple farms, an indication of relatively high population levels and a warmer climate; never have the uplands of the North York Moors been so densely populated than during this period. There are literally thousands of 'howes' throughout the Moors, ranging from small bumps to impressive raised mounds high on the moorland ridges. These howes, along with dikes (or ditches), are thought to have marked out tribal boundaries with each territory taking in a little bit of everything from high moorland, valley meadows, woodland and watercourses. As the forests disappeared, the soil was leached of nutrients and could therefore only support the hardiest of plants such as heather - the heather moors that we love so much today began with the clearance of the forests by these Bronze Age farmers. The onset of the Iron Age from 500 BC and the development of iron implements accelerated the felling of the native forests. These early Celtic tribes, known collectively as the Brigantes, also constructed more elaborate defensive earthworks as well as the first of the prehistoric hill forts, such as the strategic fort at Boltby Scar.

Unfortunately these defensive earthworks were not effective against the might of the Roman Empire. The Roman legions arrived in this far-flung corner of their Empire circa 70AD, predominantly on a military basis although they also exploited iron ore deposits. The Brigantes tribes were quickly subjugated and the Romans set about constructing a network of forts and roads to divide up the lands and exert their power over the native British. Relics of this period of Roman rule are few and far between, however the remains that do exist are truly impressive. The finest stretch of preserved Roman road in England can still be seen on Wheeldale Moor near Goathland, originally built to provide fast access between the Roman forts at York and Malton with the coast. Roman camps were built along this road at Cawthorn and Lease Rigg near Grosmont whilst a string of Signal Stations were constructed along the coast. By the end of the 4th Century Roman rule had come to an end although life for the local farmers continued much as it had done before. The period following the end of Roman rule, known as the Dark Ages, witnessed the arrival of wave after wave of settlers whose legacy can be seen throughout the area today in the form of villages, place-names, traditions, languages and dialects.

The Angles and Saxons originally came over from northern Europe and settled in this area in profusion. The North York Moors became part of the powerful Northumbrian kingdom of Deira that stretched from the Forth to the Humber (hence 'North Humber Land'). They brought with them their own culture, language and system of farming, establishing communities that were the first 'real' villages of the North York Moors, paving the way for the settlement pattern we see today. Place-names offer a good insight into the origins of a village and the suffixes 'ing', 'ley', 'ton' and 'ham' indicate an Anglo-Saxon village. It was also during this period that many of the old Pagan beliefs were swept away when a number of small religious houses were established in the 7th Century by Celtic monks in secluded locations such as Lastingham, Kirkdale, Hackness and Whitby. Scandinavians, predominantly Danes and Norwegians, arrived during the 9th and 10th centuries attacking villages and plundering churches, however, these Vikings soon settled in this area and made peace with the Anglo-Saxons. The villages and farmsteads of these Vikings invaders can be identified today through place-names such as 'by' which indicated a farm (for example 'Hawnby'). They rebuilt many churches incorporating both Anglian and Danish influences in their design and also brought with them a tradition of building that has remained through the ages. They favoured isolated locations for their farms and built 'long-houses' where barn and house were under one roof, a design still in use today. Perhaps their greatest legacy was their language, the forerunner of the Yorkshire dialect that can still be heard in some of the more remote valleys, with many common words entering the language such as rigg, dale, gill, beck and keld.

So, by the end of the 11th Century the settlement pattern of today was largely in place, the culmination of a diverse mixture of people, races, cultures, languages, rituals and customs that fused to form the underlying character of the people of this district, which still holds today.

The Norman Conquest of 1066 heralded the beginning of major change for this area. The terrible Harrying of the North in 1069 devastated many villages and put waste to large tracts of land. The lands of the old English lords were confiscated and 'given' to loyal Norman barons who subsequently built numerous castles throughout the North York Moors as a show of power, such as Helmsley,

Pickering and Cropton to name a few. However, the main legacy of this period was the monasteries, which were founded from the 12th Century onwards at Rievaulx, Byland and Whitby, with many smaller priories throughout the area including Arden, Rosedale and Grosmont; a total of twenty-five religious houses were established in this area. Monasteries such as Rievaulx Abbey became wealthy and powerful as huge tracts of land, albeit mainly poor uplands, were bestowed on them by Norman lords who believed that such gifts would help them on their way to the 'next life'. The monks successfully developed these poor lands into profitable sheep farms controlled through a network of granges, changing the land use of the North York Moors forever in the process. The monks of medieval England also developed brewing, milling, horse breeding and ironstone mining; they sowed the seeds of organised industrial and agricultural production that would continue until the onset of the Industrial Revolution. The fortunes of the monasteries took a turn for the worse during the 14th Century with frequent Scottish raids, economic recession which caused a slump in wool prices and the Black Death that wiped out much of the population.

The Dissolution of the Monasteries in the 16th Century by Henry VIII led to a major change in land ownership with the sequestration of the monastic lands by the Crown that were then 'sold' to loyal lords and landowners, although many prosperous yeoman farmers had already begun to emerge. Catholicism was slow to die in this remote corner of England and continued to be practised in many places, indeed Egton Bridge is often referred to as the 'village missed by the Reformation'. People turned to Non-Conformist faiths instead of the Church of England and even today most villages have a Methodist Chapel or Friend's Meeting House. As developments in agriculture continued throughout the 18th Century, the open communal fields and commons of medieval England began to be enclosed by stone walls and farmhouses were rebuilt as prosperity increased. A feature of the North York Moors are the vast open moorlands which were never enclosed due to the poor soils; these moors became the grouse shooting preserves of the local lords and are therefore, in many cases, still technically commons.

It is hard to believe that the Industrial Revolution had such a major impact on this seemingly rural landscape. During the 17th Century the mining of alum on the coast as well as the Cleveland Hills developed into a relatively large-scale industrial activity and soon deposits such as jet, coal and ironstone began to be mined from the hills on an ever-increasing basis. During the 18th Century communications began to improve with Turnpike roads opening and paved pannierways being built across the moors. However, it was during the early years of the 19th Century that industry really took off. Rosedale and Eskdale witnessed industrial activity on such a scale that they became almost urban environments with railways, terraced houses, spoil heaps, mine shafts and chimneys all built as a result of the booming ironstone industry. In addition to the railway around the head of Rosedale which was used to transport the ironstone to Teesside, a passenger railway was constructed between Whitby and Pickering. Before long, railways literally radiated in every possible direction from Whitby bringing new life and prosperity to this famous fishing and whaling port. These railways also brought tourists to Whitby and the inland 'resort' of Goathland. Dwindling reserves and cheaper imports led to the closure of the ironstone mines in the early 20th Century. New industries began to be exploited with the planting of the vast Cropton and Dalby Forests and the rapid growth in tourism. Millions of us now visit this area to escape our everyday lives, seek solace amongst the moors and recharge our batteries, however, the irony of this is that the things people come to see need protecting from the very same people who are in danger of destroying them due to visitor numbers (for example the daffodils of Farndale). In recent years there has been unprecedented pressure on this beautiful landscape from the countless problems created by overwhelming tourism in addition to which there are many more issues that threaten the overall 'wellbeing' of the National Park that are not linked so directly with tourism such as the state of the rural economy, thirsty cities, housing developments, communications masts, loss of heather moorland, threats to habitats...

The North York Moors National Park, designated in 1952, covers 554 square miles of incredibly diverse scenery, however it must be pointed out that it is neither national nor a park; 83% is under private ownership, 14.5% is owned by Forest Enterprise, 1.5% by the National Trust and 1% by the North York Moors National Park Authority. The National Park Authority helps the landowners, who are responsible for the management of the park, by offering advice and assistance to local people and visitors, as well as acting as a planning authority. It has two main purposes:

1. Conserve and enhance the natural beauty, wildlife and cultural heritage of the North York Moors.

2. Promote opportunities for public enjoyment and understanding of the special qualities of the National Park.

They also have a duty to foster the social and economic wellbeing of local communities.

A very difficult task indeed; it is hard to 'promote' and 'conserve' at the same time! They employ around 76 full-time and 54 part-time staff, operate Visitor Centres, a Ranger Service and work closely with conservation groups, landowners and the local community with successful schemes such as the Moorland Regeneration Programme that has been an important aspect in the maintenance of the heather moors in recent years; over 95% of the heather moors are managed in line with the National Park Authority Conservation Objectives. These moors are important as they stand as the largest remaining expanse of heather moorland in England and Wales, almost all of which have been classified as a Site of Special Scientific Interest and a Special Protection Area under the EU Birds Directive as well as a Special Area of Conservation under the EU Habitats Directive. These heather moors are almost all in the hands of various private owners who manage the heather for sheep and grouse, the mainstays of the local economy. Without this careful management there would be no heather moorland in the National Park. The heather is burnt on a rotational basis during the winter months to provide new shoots for the grouse to feed on with areas of older heather left for the birds to nest in. White quartz grit is also left in heaps on the moors for the grouse to eat to aid their digestion of the tough heather. Predators such as rats, crows, stoats and foxes that attack ground-nesting birds are controlled, and bracken is sprayed to prevent it from encroaching onto the moors and choking the heather. Between August the 12th and December 10th shooting parties 'crop' the grouse thus leaving a sustainable number of birds for the breeding season the following year, if this was not carried out many birds would not survive the winter. This shooting season also brings in valuable income for the owners of the moors as well as local pubs, hotels and shops.

Within the boundary of the National Park are over 700 ancient monuments, 41 Conservation Areas, 3,013 listed buildings, 58 Sites of Special Scientific Interest, numerous National and Local Nature Reserves, 1,408 miles of footpaths and bridleways (incidentally I walked over 650 miles of them whilst researching this book) and 26 miles of coastline that has been designated as the North Yorkshire and Cleveland Heritage Coast - and upwards of 8 million people arrive annually to admire the area's natural beauty. Tourism, farming and grouse shooting are the foundations of the local economy providing jobs for many of the 25,000 people who live within the National Park. Interestingly, Government funding for such an important part of our heritage and culture stands at £2.43 million with a further £803,000 coming from Local Authority (2000/01). On top of this the National Park Authority relies on other sources of income to enable it to carry out its work, particularly European Grants and specifically targeted Government Grants through bodies such as the Countryside Commission. Such a beautiful, varied and important part of our lives should, without question, receive the best funding it can possibly get to ensure that sustainable tourism is developed hand in hand with conservation and preservation. We must ensure that our National Parks are looked after now so that they are passed on to the next generation in good working order. Remember, when undertaking this walk: treat the countryside with care and respect, leave only footprints and take only photographs and memories.

THE GEOLOGY OF
THE NORTH YORK MOORS

. . . .

The North York Moors National Park is justly famous for its gentle valleys and rolling heather moorland across which races bracing air tinged with the salty taste of the North Sea. This scenery attracts huge numbers of visitors who come to marvel at the natural beauty, but what they are looking at is actually the culmination of millions of years of varying influences that have shaped the rocks of the North York Moors. These rocks are the foundation of everything we see, without them there would be no vegetation, building materials, valleys or scenery! Armed with a little knowledge about how the landscape evolved, the countryside through which you will walk along this route will hopefully be viewed in a new light. There are five main areas within the North York Moors National Park: the Tabular Hills to the south, Hambleton Hills to the west, Cleveland Hills to the north, the North Sea cliffs and coastline to the east and in the heart are the central heather moors. To understand how these hills, valleys and coastline were formed we need to look back to the dawn of time when the first rocks were created.

The rocks of the North York Moors are, with the exception of a narrow band of volcanic rock (known as whinstone) that runs through the heart of the moors, sedimentary rocks formed during the Jurassic period that began over 210 million years ago. The oldest are the Lias group of rocks that were formed over a 60 million year period when silts and deposits were laid down on the bed of a deep sea and were gradually compressed into thick layers of shale with some layers of ironstone and sandstone. These rocks underlie the entire North York Moors and can be seen along the coast and valley sides where the sea and rivers have eroded through the overlying rock stratas. This deep sea gradually became shallower and rivers from the Scandinavian mountains flowed into it forming a vast river delta. These rivers brought down sand, mud and silt from the mountains which were then deposited in this delta to form the sandstones of the Ravenscar

Group of rocks on top of the older Liassic shales; these sandstone rocks now form the central moorlands. Over time a warm shallow sea advanced to cover this river delta and countless tiny sea creatures fell to the seabed over millions of years to form layers of limestone, calcareous grits and clays known as the Oolite Group of rocks, which today form the Tabular and Hambleton Hills.

These different groups of rocks - Lias, Ravenscar and Oolite - formed thick bands of rocks on top of each other, however about 60 million years ago this landmass was raised out of the sea by tectonic action (the same forces that created the Alps of Europe) to form a vast domed landform that stretched from the Pennines to the North Sea. This landmass tilted slightly towards the North Sea and rivers soon carved valleys across these hills. It was the powerful action of these rivers, assisted to a large degree by the effects of ice, which created the Vale of York thus isolating the huge landmass of the North York Moors. Over millions of years the forces of nature have attacked these rocks eroding them into the landforms of today so that by the onset of the last Great Ice Age the general physical geography of the North York Moors we see today would have been more or less in place. This Ice Age lasted over a period of about 2 million years with the ice advancing and retreating on several occasions, the last retreat being about 10,000 years ago. The North York Moors was an area of frozen waste bound to the north, east and west by huge ice sheets that had flowed down from the ice caps of Scotland, the Lake District and Scandinavia. It was only towards the end of the last Ice Age that the effects of the ice were felt in this region. The retreating glaciers dropped huge amounts of boulder clay, great torrents of glacial meltwater filled many of the valleys particularly Esk Dale and the Vale of Pickering and when these lakes then overflowed incredible meltwater channels were carved out through the hills such as Newton Dale Gorge.

Over time wind, rain and ice have eroded away the top layers of rocks so that the limestone and calcareous grits of the Oolite group of rocks have gone completely from the central dome and can now only be found along the southern and western edges of the North York Moors where they form the Tabular Hills and Hambleton Hills. This erosion in the heart of the North York Moors has exposed the Ravenscar sandstone, through which rivers have cut deeply down into the underlying Lias rocks. These Liassic shales are soft and easily eroded, which has meant that the river valleys in this area are wide U-shaped valleys with rich soils. These different layers of rocks have also provided a wealth of minerals and valuable deposits which have been exploited by man since prehistoric times including ironstone, coal, jet, alum, potash, limestone and whinstone.

Helmsley

FAUNA AND FLORA

Due to the varied geology, geography and climate of the North York Moors there is an enormous diversity and abundance of plants, flowers, birds, insects and animals, most of which can be enjoyed at first hand by the observant walker.

The famed heather moorland is a very special place that is thankfully protected as a Site of Special Scientific Interest due to the number and variety of rare birds that visit or breed amongst the unique habitat of heather, grass, moss and bog plants. There are three main species of wild heather, the most common is Ling, which flowers in late summer, and the less common Bell and Cross-leaved heather which both flower several weeks earlier. The hardy bilberry bushes can often be found amongst the heather, the succulent fruit a local delicacy in home-made pies. Steps are being taken to control the bracken as it spreads at an alarming rate choking everything in its path. The upland moors are quite well-drained and therefore dry places, however there are quite a few wet areas of bog as well as some lowland wetlands such as Fen Bogs at the head of Newton Dale where the peat layer is over 40-ft deep in places. These wetlands support plants such as sphagnum moss, cotton grass, common spotted orchid, bog asphodel and the rarer insect-eating round-leaved sundew and common butterwort. They are also essential breeding grounds for numerous insects that provide food for the upland birds; it is always a pleasure to see a large dragonfly or emperor moth flying amongst the heather. In spring the moors come alive with many wonderful birds including lapwing, curlew with its very distinctive cry, golden plover, greenshank, redshank, snipe and the ubiquitous red grouse. Birds of prey such as the extremely rare merlin, peregrine falcon, short-eared owl, kestrel and the occasional common buzzard can be seen as well as several other smaller birds such as the meadow pipit, skylark and wheatear. In late summer thousands of bees swarm amongst the heather collecting pollen for the delicious heather honey, a speciality of the moors. On south-facing slopes you may also catch a glimpse of an adder, slow-worm or a common lizard, whilst across the moors you will find rabbit, hare, weasel, stoat, foxes, mice, voles and shrews.

Remnants of the primeval forest that once covered the entire North York Moors can still be found in some areas, particularly on the steep valley slopes of the Tabular Hills as well as in Esk Dale. These woods are home to a variety of deciduous trees including sessile oak, birch, wych elm, willow, mountain ash, alder and hawthorn and support a profusion of wild flowers that make these woods such a pleasure to walk through in spring with flowers such as bluebell, red campion, dog's mercury, violet, primrose, wood anemone, lady's smock, birdsfoot trefoil, common dog violet, betony, self-heal, wood sorrel, early purple orchid, ragged robin, wild garlic and foxglove a common sight. Birds such as mistle thrush, robin, wren, blue tit, great tit, coal tit, willow warbler, treecreeper, bullfinch, blackcap, woodwarbler, goldfinch, great spotted and green woodpecker are all common. Amongst the undergrowth you may see badger, squirrel, fox and roe or fallow deer. The vast coniferous plantations of the southern moors may not support as many species as the ancient oak woodlands but are nevertheless important places for many species of birds including sparrowhawk, tawny owl, redstart, goldcrest, siskin and the nocturnal nightjar.

The many rivers and streams that drain the moors support ash, alder and willow along their banks and provide the perfect habitat for the secretive otter whilst the beautiful kingfisher fishes from overhanging branches. A variety of birds live on the riverbanks and surrounding meadowland including common sandpiper, spotted flycatcher, sandmartins, grey heron, ringed plover, oystercatcher, sedge warbler, dipper, grey wagtail (or its rarer cousin the yellow wagtail), stonechat, pied wagtail, housemartin and swallow whilst barn owl, pipistrelle and long-eared bat may be seen flying across wooded fields at dusk. A variety of wild flowers and plants grow on the riverbanks and in sheltered corners away from munching sheep such as great willow-herb, purple loosestrife, meadowsweet, water aven and, of course, wild daffodils.

STAGE ONE

HELMSLEY
to
HUTTON-LE-HOLE

✦

"After walking for several hours across the flat and fertile farming country of the Vale of Pickering through attractive villages of wide grassy verges lined with old cottages, I gently climbed through the woods of Kirkdale up onto the flat plateau of the Tabular Hills and the twin villages of Fadmoor and Gillamoor. Unexpectedly, the road turned sharply down Broom Hill to reveal a surprise. There it was at last, a foretaste of the next five days and the reason for this walk and my raison d'être. From my vantage point on this wooded ridge I looked out across the lush pastures of lower Farndale with the River Dove leisurely threading its way through a jumble of fields dotted with the occasional farmhouse. But the real thrill was the heather-clad ridges of the central moorland stretching away into the distance. I felt as though I had deserved this view, a reward for having walked from the Vale up to the edge of the moors. And the anticipation of what lay ahead welled up inside."

Mark Reid
August 1999

WALK INFORMATION

. . . .

Points of interest: Helmsley's 'impregnable' castle, a thatched inn, the Vale of Pickering, Kirkdale's Saxon Minster, forest tracks, hidden mills, a Surprise View and arguably the prettiest village in England.

Distance:

Helmsley to Wombleton	6 miles
Wombleton to Hutton-le-Hole	8 miles
Total	14 miles

Time: Allow 7 hours

Terrain: The section from Helmsley to Kirkdale predominantly follows riverside and field paths, with some stretches along quiet country lanes; many of the fields have crops in summer. The section through Kirkdale follows forest tracks and paths up through the valley, which can be very muddy after rain. There is a fairly steep climb out of this valley up across a steep wooded bank, before a path meanders across fields over several stiles to reach Fadmoor. A quiet lane then leads to Gillamoor and down to reach Gillamoor Mill in the lower reaches of Farndale. The final part of this walk heads across a small area of moorland (boggy in places) before dropping down into Hutton-le-Hole. Easy walking terrain all of the way with no significant climbs - gently does it on the first day!

The riverside paths alongside the River Rye and Hodge Beck may be muddy and/or flooded after very heavy rain. In particular, the riverside path between Helmsley and the Fish Farm is prone to flooding after heavy rain and the meandering riverbank is also being slowly eroded away in places.* There are some stretches of road walking along quiet country lanes, as *well as the A170 to cross at Welburn. The climb out of Sleightholme Dale is quite steep. Many of the paths and tracks are muddy underfoot, and there are numerous stiles to cross along the way.*

* If the riverside path along the banks of the River Rye between Helmsley and the Fish Farm is flooded and impassable, then either follow the footpath on the north side of the river/dismantled railway from Helmsley to join the road to the north-west of Harome (SE 634 827) or follow the road from Helmsley to Harome. OS Explorer map OL26 required for these alternative routes.

Ascents: Sleightholme Dale to Fadmoor: 175 metres

Viewpoints: A string of attractive villages and buildings add interest, with St Gregory's Minster of particular note.
Views across Sleightholme Dale from the track through the woods of Kirkdale.
'Surprise View' offers a taste of things to come with the valley of Farndale framed by heather moorland.

FACILITIES

· ·

Helmsley	Inn / B&B / Shop / P.O. / Café / Bus / Phone / Toilets / Info / YH
Harome	Inn / B&B / Shop / Bus / Phone
Wombleton	Inn / B&B / Bus / Phone
Welburn	Phone / Bus
Fadmoor	Inn / Bus / Phone
Gillamoor	Inn / B&B / Bus / Phone
Hutton-le-Hole	Inn / B&B / Shop / Café / Bus / Phone / Toilets / Info

ROUTE DESCRIPTION

. . . .

(Map One)

Starting from the Feversham Memorial in Helmsley Market Place, leave Helmsley along the A170 towards Thirsk (Bridge Street) and follow this road down over the bridge across the River Rye on the edge of Helmsley. Immediately after the bridge, take the FP to the left (SP 'Rye House') through a gate, after which bear to the right slightly across the middle of the field to reach a kissing-gate (to right of the telegraph poles) in the far right-hand corner of the field beside a sharp bend in the river. After the kissing-gate, follow the riverside path curving round to the left around this sharp bend in the river (along the foot of the steep wooded bank) then, after a short distance, head up a couple of rough steps to the right heading up across the wooded riverbank - the path quickly levels out and leads straight on across the wooded riverbank, with the River Rye just down to your left. Follow this riverside path straight on for 0.3 miles all the way to reach a kissing-gate at the end of the woods, after which continue straight on across wooded pastures, keeping close to the riverbank - *ignore any sheep tracks that branch off up to the right.* Continue along the riverside path, passing a ford then follow the river as it swings sharply round to the left. Do not follow the river all the way round to the left, but branch off to the right heading straight on across the field (alongside the fence on your right) to re-join the river again, thus cutting off a large meander in the river. Follow this riverside path downstream (river on your left) for 300 yards to reach a large FB across the River Rye near the Fish Farm (SE 632 821).

Cross the FB then turn left along a grassy track (River Rye on your left and the Fish Farm on your right) heading back upstream to join a clear lane after the Fish Farm ponds and buildings. Head straight on along this lane for a short distance then, as the lane bends up to the right, head along the grassy track to the left through a gate (actually on the bend) to run alongside the River Rye (heading back upstream) across a field to soon reach a stile beside a gate across your path (with the river to your left). After the gate, carry straight on across the field (with the river to your left) then, where the field narrows as you reach the other side of the field, carry straight on along this narrow section then head sharp right under an old railway bridge through the old railway embankment. After the railway bridge, head straight up the field alongside the fence on your right to a gate and the road (SE 634 827). Turn right along the road *(take care)* for 0.75 miles until you come to a road bridge across the River Riccal. Turn right immediately before this bridge and cross the stile by a gate (SP), then head immediately left and walk across two fields (keeping close to the river on your left) then follow the river round to the left to reach a stile beside a gate just behind an old corrugated metal shed. After the stile, head straight on along the clear path for a short distance then left over a bridge across the River Riccal after which follow the enclosed path round to join the road next to a pond in the centre of Harome (SE 646 820).

Turn left along the road then, at the road junction, head straight on towards 'Wombleton, Nunnington' *(Star Inn short detour to the left at this road junction)* and follow the road through the village then, just before you leave the village, turn left along Back Lane (at the thatched cottage). Follow this lane for a short distance then, as it bends to the left, head straight on through two gates (SP) and follow the path alongside the hedge on your left up across two large fields. At the top of the second field, cross the stile ahead in the corner of the field and follow the path through dense trees/undergrowth which soon leads out onto a field. As you emerge out onto the field, head to the left across the field (cutting the corner off the field) to reach a small gate in the fence/hedge along the top of the field, after which head straight on up alongside a hedge on your right then, as you reach Shaw Moor Farm, follow the enclosed path passing to the right of the buildings and onto a road (SE 650 833).

(Map Two)

Turn right along the farm road and follow this for almost 0.5 miles to reach a T-junction where you turn left along the road (Gale Lane), then take the first turning to the right after 0.25 miles (SP) along Sykehead Lane (private farm lane). Follow this lane straight on for 0.5 miles to reach Syke House Farm on your left. Just after the farm buildings turn off the lane along the FP to the left over a stile by a gate and then through a kissing-gate beside another gate just beyond, after which head straight down the field alongside the fence/hedge on your left to quickly reach another kissing-gate beside a gate in the field corner, then head to the right down across the middle of the field to reach another kissing-gate in the fence to your right at the bottom of Syke Wood (where the field levels out, halfway down the field). After the kissing-gate, head straight on with the woods on your right to reach two stiles either side of a small stream (Syke Cut), after which bear left across the field to reach another stile in the field corner. After this stile, head left along the perimeter of the field then round to the right after a short distance (following the field perimeter) alongside the hedge on your left, which you follow until you come to a small gate in the hedge on your left *(houses of Wombleton just ahead)*. Go through the gate and head straight on *(ignore gate to your right)* alongside the trees/fence on your right to reach a stile in the field corner just before a brick-built barn that leads onto a short section of enclosed path which quickly takes you onto a grassy track (Back Lane) beside this brick-built barn. Follow this enclosed grassy track straight on passing behind the houses/gardens of Wombleton on your right. After a while, the grassy track becomes a lane which you follow straight on then round to the right to reach the main road at the top end of Wombleton village (SE 668 842).

Turn right along the main road through the village then take the turning to the left at the pub along Page Lane (SP 'Village Hall' and 'Welburn, Kirkbymoorside') and almost immediately follow the lane to the left (SP) opposite the pub car park that leads up to reach the Sports Field. Turn right along the boundary of the Sports Field, over a stile then head straight on across the next large field and through a large gap in an old hedge across your path at the end of this field, after which continue straight on alongside the hedge on your left all the way down to reach the road at Welburn (SE 680 847). At the road take the FP opposite (SP) and head straight on along the edge of the field (alongside the metal fence on your right) to soon reach the corner of the field *(ignore the stile in this corner)* where you head left across the field *(same field as you have just been walking across)* alongside the fence/wooded banks of Hodge Beck on your right all the way to reach a stile beside a small gate in the corner of the field that leads onto a lane beside Tilehouse Bridge across Hodge Beck. Cross the stone wall-stile opposite *(do not cross the bridge)* and head straight across the field to reach the main road (A170).

Cross the road *(take care)* and follow the FP opposite over a stile in the hedge/fence, after which head straight on across the field keeping close to the edge of the field on your right passing between the old railway bridge across to your left and the railway viaduct on your right to reach the road at St Gregory's Minster (SE 677 856). Cross the road and follow the lane opposite to reach the church. Continue along the track passing to the left of the church, through a gate then follow the grassy track straight on across the field to a FB across Hodge Beck, after which head straight on along the grassy track up across the field to a gate that leads into woodland (Kirkdale Wood East).* Follow the track up through Kirkdale Wood East (with Hodge Beck down to your left) to soon reach a junction of paths and tracks, where you follow the (level) path to the left which heads along the bottom of the wooded bank (with the bottom edge of the woods to your left) gently meandering through the woods for 0.25 miles (heading up through Kirkdale) to join a clear forest track again alongside Hodge Beck. Follow this track straight on gradually climbing uphill (Hodge Beck down to your left) then down to reach the bridge and old mill at Hold Caldron (SE 668 869).

NB: the FB across Hodge Beck was washed away during the floods of June 2005 and at the time of updating this Second Edition (March 2010) had not been replaced, although there are plans to do so in the near future. The river is usually easy to cross as there is an adjacent ford and the riverbed is almost always dry; however, in times of flood follow this alternative route: as you reach the road just before St Gregory's Minster, turn right down the road and over a ford/FB across Hodge Beck, immediately after which take the FP to the left. Follow the undulating path across the steep wooded riverbank (river down to your left) then, where the river bends away to the left, head up to join a wide forest path. Turn left along this wide path down to join the track through Kirkdale Wood East.

Continue straight on along the track *(do not cross the bridge)* for a short distance then, where the track forks, follow the left-hand track straight on through a gate. After the gate, walk straight on along the track across the middle of the open field heading up through the valley of Kirkdale, with Hodge Beck just across to your left. The track soon joins the fence/edge of the forest on your right - carry straight on along this track heading up through Kirkdale for 0.25 miles to join the river (Hodge Beck) on your left in a fairly narrow section of the valley. Continue along the track through this narrow section (still with the bottom edge of the forest on your right), which soon opens out into a narrow field (river bends away slightly to your left). Continue straight on along the track across this narrow field for about 250 yards then, at the end of this field at the overgrown hedge/line of trees across your path, take the path to the right over a stile by a gate that leads up into the woods. This wide path quickly levels out and leads straight on along the bottom of the steep wooded hillside (Brockhill Hagg), with the edge of the woods to your left, heading up through the valley for 0.5 miles *(this wide path becomes a track)* to eventually reach a gate across the track (SE 662 880). Immediately after the gate, branch off the track to the left along a path that leads alongside the fence/edge of the woods on your left *(ignore stile to left and the sunken track rising up through the woods)* for approx. 200 yards to join a clear forest track. Follow this track up through the woods for approx. 250 yards then, where the track bends away to the right, head through the small gate in the fence just off to the left that leads out onto a field. Walk up across the field to the right to a gate in the top far corner of the field that leads onto a clear woodland track. Follow this track straight on for 0.5 miles all the way to reach Sleightholme Dale Road (SE 665 891).

Turn left along the road passing Sleightholme Dale Lodge (with its high garden wall) and on to reach Aumery Park Farm after just under 0.5 miles. As you reach the farm buildings turn right back on yourself through a gate (SP 'Fadmoor') and follow the path up across the hillside (passing to the left of the telegraph pole) to join a clear path that leads quite steeply up through woodland to the top of Urn

Bank. As you reach the top of the bank (with the fence and edge of the woodland just in front of you) follow the path to the right (waymarker) along the top of Urn Bank for approx. 100 yards then cross the stile to the left hidden in undergrowth (waymarker post) that leads out onto fields. After the stile, follow the path diagonally to the right across the middle of the field to a stile in the hedge to your right (halfway up the field), after which head to the left across the next field over another stile set in the hedge/fence then straight on across the field to another stile in a hedge/fence. After this stile, bear to the right across the field to a stile towards the far right-hand corner *(rooftops of Fadmoor in the distance)*, after which turn left heading across the middle of the narrow field to reach a stile over the fence/hedge to your right halfway across this field. After this stile, head left across the middle of the field and over another stile over the hedge on the opposite side towards the corner of the field, after which turn left to a gate in the corner of the field that leads onto the road (near to some farm buildings) on the outskirts of Fadmoor (SE 674 895). Turn right along the road into Fadmoor then left along the road across the village green towards 'Gillamoor, Farndale'.

(Map Three)

Follow the road out of Fadmoor and continue along the road for 0.5 miles to reach Gillamoor, where you continue straight on along the road through the village to reach the church where you follow the main road passing to the left side of the church and churchyard to quickly reach 'Surprise View' at the end of the churchyard, where the road bends sharply down to the left *(marked by an inscribed stone tablet set into the wall)*. As you reach Surprise View, follow the tree-shaded road steeply down to the left for 0.25 miles then, as you near the bottom of the hill, take the stony track back on yourself to the right. Follow this track straight on for 0.25 miles then bending left down to reach Gillamoor Mill. As you approach the mill the track forks - follow the left-hand track down alongside the hedge on your left then, as you reach the mill buildings, turn left along a track and follow this skirting to the left around the mill buildings to reach a FB across the River Dove beyond the mill (SE 687 904).

Cross the FB and head straight up two fields alongside the hedge on your right towards Grouse Hall (farm). As you reach the top of the second field (just before Grouse Hall), cross the stile to the right in the field corner then head up across the middle of the field to reach a stile by a large tree then head straight on across the next field bearing slightly to the right to reach a stile and FB across a stream in the far right-hand corner of the field that leads up to a track. Turn left along the track for a few paces then branch off to the right along a narrow path (just before the telegraph poles) through bracken and heather gradually climbing up to join a wider grassy path at the top of the bank which you follow straight on for approx. 100 yards to reach a fork in the path (waymarker). Follow the right-hand path that leads straight on gently meandering across the heather/bracken moorland *(keep to the clear, wide path)* for 0.25 miles to reach a kissing-gate set in a wall/fence (SE 699 906). After the kissing-gate, follow the enclosed path straight on down towards Hutton-le-Hole for 0.25 miles to reach a track across your path. Cross straight over the track through the kissing-gate opposite, then head straight on across the field alongside the fence on your right to reach another kissing-gate in the field corner, where you head through this gate onto the other side of the fence/hedge. Follow this fence straight on (now on your left) bearing round then down to reach a gate that leads onto the road at the top of Hutton-le-Hole (SP). Turn right along the road into the village.

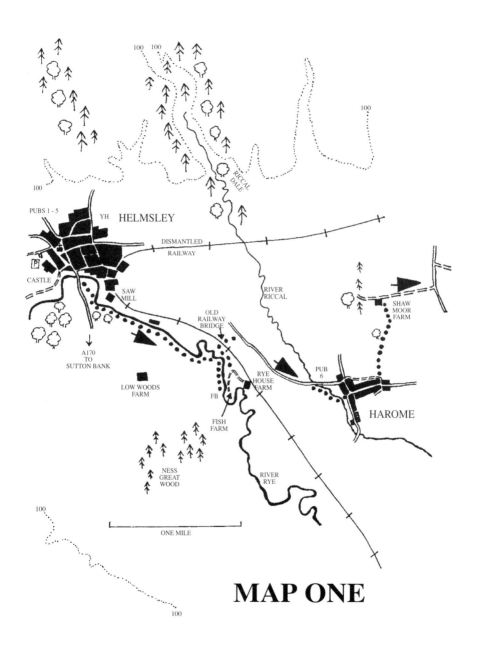

MAP ONE

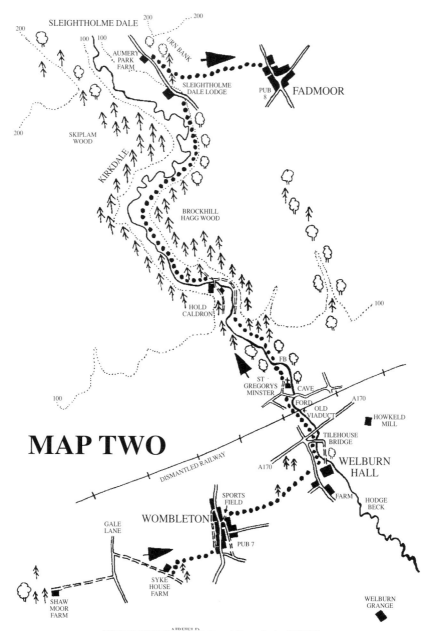

SLEIGHTHOLME DALE

200

200

200

200

100 100

100

200

URN BANK

AUMERY
PARK
FARM

SLEIGHTHOLME
DALE LODGE

PUB
8

FADMOOR

SKIPLAM
WOOD

KIRKDALE

BROCKHILL
HAGG WOOD

100

HOLD
CALDRON

100

FB

ST
GREGORYS
MINSTER

CAVE

FORD

OLD
VIADUCT

A170

HOWKELD
MILL

MAP TWO

DISMANTLED RAILWAY

A170

TILEHOUSE
BRIDGE

WELBURN
HALL

SPORTS
FIELD

FARM

HODGE
BECK

GALE
LANE

WOMBLETON

PUB 7

SYKE
HOUSE
FARM

SHAW
MOOR
FARM

WELBURN
GRANGE

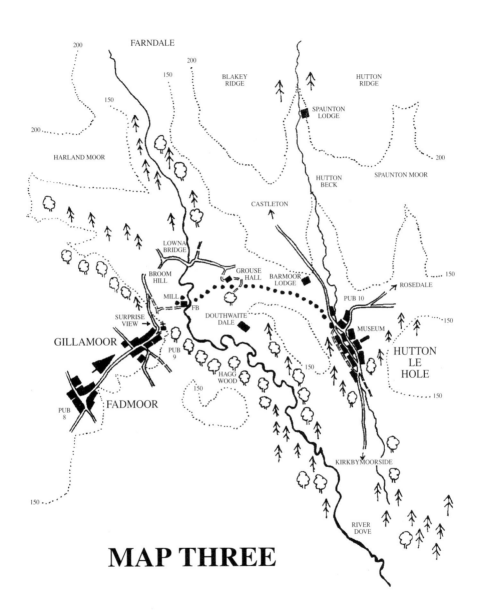

FARNDALE

200

200

150

BLAKEY
RIDGE

HUTTON
RIDGE

150

SPAUNTON
LODGE

200

HARLAND MOOR

200

HUTTON
BECK

SPAUNTON MOOR

CASTLETON

LOWNA
BRIDGE

BROOM
HILL

GROUSE
HALL

BARMOOR
LODGE

ROSEDALE

150

MILL

FB

PUB 10

150

SURPRISE
VIEW

DOUTHWAITE
DALE

MUSEUM

150

GILLAMOOR

PUB
9

HUTTON
LE
HOLE

HAGG
WOOD

150

150

FADMOOR

150

PUB
8

150

KIRKBYMOORSIDE

150

RIVER
DOVE

MAP THREE

HELMSLEY can truly be described as the 'Gateway to the Moors' as several busy roads converge on its Market Place, which is always crowded with visitors who seem compelled to stop and stretch their legs when they catch sight of the imposing Victorian monument to the second Lord Feversham, built to a design by Sir Gilbert Scott. This elegant North Riding market town is the first taste for many people of the North York Moors, and what an introduction! Helmsley sets the standard for the next six days, and if this is the benchmark then the North York Moors must be a magical place. Whenever I cross the bridge and drive into the Market Place my heart lifts as this town marks the start of relaxation and the end of worries as from here northwards lies some of the finest countryside in England. *"Helmsley is one of those little market towns which one can find nowhere in the world but in England. There is a market square, there is an old castle, there are old houses and old-fashioned inns; tall elms stand sentinel above human habitations, and a murmuring stream runs through the town to lose itself in the Rye."* **(J. S. Fletcher 'The Enchanting North' 1908).**

It was a Saxon called Helm who first made a clearing in the vast forest for his small farm and by the time of the Norman survey there were several families living here in what was known as Elmeslac. The town's development as a bustling market centre began in earnest following the establishment of nearby Rievaulx Abbey in 1132 and the rebuilding of a stronger stone castle. A weekly market charter was granted in 1672, however, regular markets had been held here for centuries as the old market cross testifies. This used to be situated within the churchyard before it was moved to its present location in the Market Place as in medieval times markets were often held on the Sabbath and within church grounds as many people had to make long journeys to church. The tower of All Saints Church with its four pinnacles rises above the rooftops, a place of worship since Saxon times although the original stone Norman church was almost completely rebuilt in the 1860s with the exception of the wonderful Norman doorway. Inside are many items of interest including a yoke taken from the neck of an African slave in the 19th Century, medieval pikes once used by the local constabulary to subdue unruly inhabitants and oak furniture crafted by 'Mousey' Thompson of Kilburn. Before the Dissolution of the Monasteries in the 16th Century All Saints' was administered by Augustinian Canons from Kirkham. Adjacent to the church stands the vicarage, a magnificent half-timbered house known as Canons Garth that was originally built by the monks of Kirkham. Helmsley's most famous vicar was Rev. Gray who made an everlasting impression on the community when he served the Parish between 1870 and 1913. This redoubtable man embarked on many 'social' campaigns which he saw as an integral part of Christian living including the conditions of the workhouse, cleanliness of the water supply, the state of the town's roads and paths, the dangers of women's corsets and improving children's health, although he was not so tolerant of other denominations. He saw his role as being almost 'lord' of the manor and chastised people, including Lord Feversham, who did not consult him over matters concerning the town. Another aspect of Helmsley's development was the production of linen and woollen products that became an important cottage industry, indeed many weavers' cottages can still be found in the town and the small bridge behind the Town Hall is known as Dyers Bridge as this was where they used to dye the cloth in the stream.

Helmsley is well worth exploring to discover the mixture of elegant Georgian buildings, a handful of medieval houses, old cottages and coaching inns. Dominating the Market Place is the Town Hall, built in 1901 by Lord Feversham as a court house and market hall, however, it was given to the town in 1958 and now houses the Library. Interesting shops and old-fashioned inns line the many lanes that lead off the Market Place, which will eventually take you to the prettiest part of Helmsley along Castlegate with the crystal-clear Borough Beck flowing between the houses. Look out for the former Blacksmiths along Borogate as well as old stabling blocks that once belonged to a coaching inn and are now home to a riding school. Tucked behind houses off Bridge Street is an old Friends' Meeting House, now used as an arts centre, whilst an old Victorian workhouse, now known as Woodard House, dating from 1861 can still be found along High Street. During the 18th Century Helmsley developed as an important overnight centre for stagecoaches. The famous Black Swan Hotel has been welcoming visitors since at least the 18th Century and once boasted a direct stagecoach route to London. This hotel incorporates three distinct buildings with the original inn on the far right, a fine Georgian house in the middle and a half timbered Tudor house to the left that once housed the Earl of Rutland's Agents and was then used as the Rectory. Several old inns and alehouses have closed over the years including the Golden Lion Inn, situated in the corner of the Market Place next to the old Police Station and now occupied by Nicholson's butcher's shop. Along Castlegate stands a half timbered Manor House that was also an inn where William Wordsworth and his sister stayed in 1802 when they passed through the town on their way to visit William's future bride near Scarborough, although some claim that they stayed at the Black Swan.

Dominating the town are the impressive ruins of Helmsley Castle, which date back to 1120 when Walter Espec, the son of a Norman lord, was given a vast tract of land by Henry I who wanted to strengthen his northern kingdom against the unruly Scots. Only the impressive double defensive earthworks remain of this original wooden castle as his brother-in-law Robert de Roos rebuilt the castle in stone in late 12th Century. The castle was again strengthened in the 13th Century with the addition of the north and south Barbicans and modifications to the earthworks. *"It is thought to have been begun by Walter Espec, a warrior with jet black hair, piercing eyes, and a voice like a trumpet. He was one of the leaders in the Battle of the Standard in 1138, but was really a man of peace, for he founded the abbeys of Rievaulx and Kirkham."* **(A. Mee, 'Yorkshire North Riding' 1941)**. Over the centuries the de Roos family grew wealthy and powerful through marriage and became known as Lord Ros of Helmsley and Belvoir (Roos lost an 'o' in the intervening years!) with estates in the East Midlands as well as Yorkshire. In 1525 Lord Ros of Helmsley was awarded the Earldom of Rutland due to his support of the Tudor dynasty which later enabled him to purchase the buildings and estates of Rievaulx at a very favourable price following their suppression by

Henry VIII. It was during this time that the more refined living quarters of the mansion hall were built within the castle walls. Through marriage the estates and title passed in the early 17th Century to George Villiers, the Duke of Buckingham, however, in 1689 on the death of the Duke of Buckingham the castle and its estates were bought by wealthy London banker Sir Charles Duncombe whose descendants, the Earls of Feversham, still own the castle. The draughty castle was replaced in 1713 by Duncombe Park, a fine stately home famous for its landscaped gardens and terraces. During its heyday the castle was renowned throughout the country for its impregnability due to the many innovative defensive features incorporated into the design, including the double earthworks, barbicans, high curtain walls and famous D-shaped tower. The castle, however, never saw any action until the English Civil War when Parliamentarian forces under Sir Thomas Fairfax besieged its Royalist garrison under the command of Colonel Crossland in 1644, who surrendered only when supplies ran out after Royalist reinforcements were intercepted. When the troops did surrender they were allowed to march out of the castle with their small arms (and their dignity), indeed many troops promptly changed sides and joined the Parliamentarians! The castle was made untenable under Cromwell's orders, and the D-shaped East Tower was blown apart; I recommend a tour of the castle, if only to see the dramatic defensive earthworks.

The first part of *The Inn Way* follows the River Rye through lower Ryedale; Helmsley marks the point where the deep valley of Ryedale opens out into the flat Vale of Pickering and provides a reminder of the contrast between this fertile plain and the harsher North York Moors for the rest of your walk. The River Rye is an absolute delight along this stretch as it meanders across farmland with countless sandmartins darting in and out of holes along the riverbank. The route also crosses and re-crosses the old railway line of the branch loop between Pickering and the Malton to York line. This railway once provided an important pulse of life for the market towns of Helmsley and Kirkbymoorside but lack of passengers meant that it succumbed to closure in 1953, a full ten years before the Beeching Report. Note the superb viaduct and bridge near Welburn.

HAROME, pronounced 'hair-rum', means 'settlement amongst the stones' and was first settled by Anglo-Saxon farmers. Harome has since matured into an attractive village with several old cruck-framed cottages lining the well-kept street, a small mill pond with noisy ducks and a Victorian church. Although many village names can be traced back to the Anglo-Saxons, the layout we see today of these villages stem from medieval times. Harome is no exception and retains its medieval layout with cottages set back from a single main street with narrow enclosed strips of land, or crofts, leading back from the houses and a second 'back lane' running behind these crofts that gives access to the larger communal 'outfields'. These outfields would have been worked by peasant farmers on a rigg and furrow basis, with the narrow crofts allocated to individual farmers who built their single storey thatched homes at the 'street end'. The lord of the manor kept a watchful eye on these peasants; indeed, a thatched Elizabethan Manor House that boasts the tallest oak crucks in the North of England was moved from the village in 1970 stone by stone and rebuilt at the Ryedale Folk Museum at Hutton-le-Hole. The cruck-frame method of construction was probably introduced into the North East by Danish invaders 1,500 years ago. In Medieval times a busy road known as Meregate came this way from Fadmoor, at the foot of the road over Rudland Rigg, via Harome and then up to join Sperragate, another ancient road that ran from Helmsley up to the old Drovers' Road at Sutton Bank. Of particular interest is the beautiful thatched pub known as the Star Inn that was reputedly built by monks in the 14th Century as a hostelry between the abbeys of Whitby and York. Inside is a glimpse of the past with low oak beams, stone flagged floor, 'Mousey' Thompson furniture and the crucks visible in the coffee loft.

WOMBLETON was first settled by a Saxon farmer called Wynnbeald although its layout, like neighbouring Harome, dates from the early medieval rebuilding of settlements following the Harrying of the North by the Normans. This is a classic linear village with crofts running from the main street leading to a back lane and 'outfields'. Its narrow single street is lined with an assortment of attractive cottages and well-tended gardens as well as the Plough Inn, part of which is housed in a 15th Century cruck-framed cottage. There is no church here as the village is served by St Gregory's Minster at Kirkdale, as it has been for over 1,400 years! Just outside the village is a disused Second World War airfield, one of many in the North East that were built on the flat vales of York and Pickering from where bombing raids were carried out over Germany. One sad consequence of these airfields are the numerous church memorials throughout the North York Moors to airmen killed when their planes crashed whilst trying to return to base.

WELBURN is dominated by the imposing Welburn Hall, a fine building hidden by trees that comes as a surprise as you approach it along the field-paths from Wombleton. The original Jacobean hall (1603) was all but destroyed by two disastrous fires over a century ago, although one 17th Century wing remains; the hall was rebuilt in the Jacobean style in 1891 following the worst fire and is now used as a school. *"Inside and out all is now decay, from the spacious kitchen with its fireplace of fourteen feet span, its old oak staircases and corridors, to the towering chimneys outside, and we ask ourselves the question – whose will be the magic hand to recall its latent beauty?"* (**G. Frank 'Ryedale and North Yorkshire Antiquities' 1888.**) In medieval times Welburn was at the heart of a busy network of roads including Thurklisti, an ancient route that connected Stokesley in the north with York via moorland roads through Bransdale and Welburn. Tilehouse Bridge, now a quiet back road spanning the diminutive Hodge Beck, was built in the 18th Century and formed part of this network of roads; whilst leaning over the parapet I glimpsed the blue flash of a kingfisher. Rievaulx Abbey held lands in the area controlled by a grange, indeed a farm nearby still bears the name Welburn Grange.

From Welburn our route turns towards the gently rising shelf of land of the Tabular Hills as we head for the high ground of the North York Moors, although the gradual ascent through sylvan Kirkdale somewhat masks the grandeur of these hills. It is only when you come to a 'nab' on the north facing escarpment that the full glory of the Tabular Hills are realised - just wait until you reach Gillamoor!

St. Gregory's Minster

ST GREGORY'S MINSTER is one of the ecclesiastical treasures of England. Few places compare to the serenity of its setting or the pleasing simplicity of its architecture; it exudes the 'spirit' of worship from the dawn of Christianity. A church has stood on this site since the 7th Century, a monastic 'mission house', or Minster (from the Latin 'monasterium'), from where the monks of either Whitby or Lastingham could spread the word of the Lord. These monks had originally travelled down to Yorkshire from Lindisfarne, the very cradle of Christianity in this country. Attacked by marauding Danes and Vikings in the 9th and 10th centuries, the church lay in ruins until the mid 11th Century when it was rebuilt. The stonemasons of 1,000 years ago incorporated a sundial into their new church, which remains as the most complete surviving Saxon inscription in the world. It reads: *"Orm Gamalsuna bohte Sanctus Gregorius Minster thonne hit wes ael tobrocan and tofalan and he hit let macan newan from grunde Christe and Sanctus Gregorius in Eadward Dagum cyning and in Tosti dagum Eorl. And Hawarth me wrohte and Brand priest. This is daeges solmerca aet ilcum tide."* This is translated as follows: *"Orm, son of Gamel bought St Gregory's church when it was completely broken and fallen down, and he had it made anew from the ground to Christ and to St Gregory, in the days of king Edward and in the days of Earl Tostig. Hawarth made me: and Brand was the priest. This is the day's sun-marker at every hour".* The inscription can be easily understood and sounds, when read quickly out loud, very similar to the local dialect we hear today in the North York Moors for this is Northumbrian English of pre-Conquest Yorkshire. With so much detail it is possible to date the rebuilding to between the years 1055 and 1065 as King Edward refers to Edward the Confessor, and Earl Tostig (Earl of Northumberland) was the brother of King Harold II, the last Anglo-Saxon king of England. The person who rebuilt the ruined church was a man named Orm, a wealthy local landowner and the descendent of a Viking who had settled in the area, which is slightly ironic considering his ancestors were probably responsible for its ransacking in the first place. It is also interesting to note that there were only eight hours in the Saxon day! Much remains of this 11th Century church, although a north aisle was added in the 13th Century and later a chancel and small tower were added in the 19th Century. Inside, look out for the original Saxon doorway that now leads into the bell tower as well as 8th Century tombs and a 13th Century font, whilst outside are several Saxon crossheads from the original church incorporated in the walls of the 11th Century rebuilding. A thought-provoking place indeed.

Across the river from the church, just off the road beside the ford, lies Kirkdale Cave. In 1821 quarrymen working the limestone out-crops found an opening in the rock-face, inside which they discovered a large amount of bones. These bones were brought to the attention of William Buckland, Professor of Geology at Oxford University, who identified them as belonging to lion, elephant, tiger, bear, hippopotamus, mammoth, rhinoceros, wolf plus the remains of hundreds of hyenas. This caused a sensation at the time and was hailed as proof of the Biblical Flood. It was in fact a hyena's den dating back over 70,000 years, long before the last Ice Age, when the area was covered by a tropical swamp. The onset of the last Ice Age meant that these animals migrated south leaving the remains of their prey to be preserved by ice and then submerged by the glacial meltwaters that once filled the Vale of Pickering. A scramble up slippery rocks takes you up the quarry face into a narrow slit that leads into the caves. *"The cave has since been partly demolished, but can still be traced by those who have a taste for the macabre. Even today a strange aura hovers over this gorge and over the lonely little church and its green churchyard – a sense of immemorial antiquity, of mystery and foreboding, and I never pass that way without feeling it."* **(A. J. Brown 'Fair North Riding' 1952).**

KIRKDALE cuts a deep, narrow course through the otherwise gently sloping shelf of limestone and calcareous sandstone that form the Tabular Hills. Hodge Beck, the diminutive stream that flows through this valley, rises several miles to the north on the flanks of Greenhow Moor near Round Hill, the highest point on the North York Moors. This stream initially flows down through Bransdale then Sleightholme Dale and finally Kirkdale before joining the River Dove in the Vale of Pickering; Hodge Beck is unique as it flows through three different dales all in the same valley! Incidentally, Sleightholme means 'flat ground near water' in Old Norse, an apt name indeed for this stretch of the valley is wide enough to allow some farms and meadowland. The steep valley sides of Kirkdale are cloaked with trees, predominantly coniferous, which are home to thousands of young pheasants reared for shooting especially in Brockhill Hagg Wood; the word 'Hagg' comes from the Old English word meaning a coppiced wood.

Hidden in the heart of Kirkdale lies Hold Caldron, a picturesque old corn mill that has a romantic setting beside Hodge Beck. The small stone bridge provides an ideal place to rest weary legs and admire the tumbling stream complete with weir as well as the attractive stone buildings; this bridge also marks the southern boundary of the North York Moors National Park. Just after Hold Caldron, Hodge Beck disappears through subterranean passages in the limestone bedrock reappearing again at Howkeld Mill near

Welburn. The bed is dry for most of the year, although during the winter a storm can suddenly bring life to the 'over-ground' river with water up to three feet deep flowing across the ford near Kirkdale Cave. There is a labyrinth of caves and passages beneath the ground here stretching for miles. According to local legend a goose once walked between Kirkdale and Kirkbymoorside through these caves without seeing the light of day, when it re-appeared it was featherless but not quite oven ready! *To the student of antiquity, and the lover of nature, this secluded spot will alike prove a welcome resort. The woods clad in leafy verdure rise abruptly on each side of the valley, at the south end of which stands the quaint old Church; no dwelling strikes the eye, no sound the ear, excepting when the swollen waters fill the otherwise dry bed of the stream beneath the walls of the church-yard...*" **(G. Frank 1888.)**

FADMOOR is an unspoilt village lying on the flat plateau of the Tabular Hills. The emphasis is still very much on agriculture, as it has been since a Saxon chief called Fadda settled here. Several working farms, including one specialising in organic produce, look out across the slightly unkempt village green which boasts a Millennium Cross carved with the dates 1823 and 2000, continuing the tradition of moorland crosses that can be traced back well over 1,000 years. Fadmoor lies at the foot of Rudland Rigg, one of several high ridges of land that run north to south through the heart of the North York Moors. The road along Rudland Rigg was an important route in medieval times and remains today as an unsurfaced track for much of the way. The Tabular Hills are predominantly made up of gently sloping limestone hills that lack surface water and therefore many villages in the area relied on ponds for water, which often ran dry. The ingenious answer to this problem was an ambitious system of watercourses to bring water from the moors. In 1747 a local man Joseph Foord skilfully engineered a narrow clay-lined channel from Ouse Gill to the north of Fadmoor that brought water to both Fadmoor and Gillamoor using gravity. An easy task you may think, but you may have noticed that there is a 200-ft escarpment in the way where the Tabular Hills fall away towards the central moors. Foord successfully devised the watercourse to take advantage of the natural tilt of the escarpment towards the coast and by doing so found a place at the foot of the escarpment that was higher than the villages. Other villages in the area wanted their own water supply and before long several watercourses had been constructed; although no longer used, many can still be traced.

GILLAMOOR, like its smaller cousin less than a mile away, was named after a Saxon called Getlingas who owned a large tract of open land in the area. There is a buzz of activity in this village with school, Post Office, well-stocked shop *(sadly, Post Office and shop closed in 2004),* great old-fashioned inn overlooking the narrow village green and a Methodist Church built in 1867 and still in use. Possibly the most unusual structure in the village is the sundial, erected in 1800 by public subscription. This solar timepiece boasts four faces on top of which is a fifth circular sundial, making it the most elaborate sundial in the country. At the far end of the village stands the unassuming St Aidan's Church, a place of worship since the 12th Century. The church we see today was entirely rebuilt in 1802 by one man, James Smith of Farndale, a 'sound workman' as the inscription declares, although faith and dedication to God probably played a part as well. The church has an exposed location on the edge of an escarpment and was therefore designed to withstand the many strong winds that howl down the valley, look carefully and you will notice that there are no windows in the north or east walls - there was no such thing as double glazing two hundred years ago! Just outside the churchyard is a large stone cross, erected to the memory of the local men who went to France to fight for this country during the First World War; a poignant reminder of the futility of war and a sad moment to reflect on just how far from home some of these men were when they died.

Where the road turns steeply down to the left near the church, a magnificent view opens out before you; this is the famous Surprise View. A tablet set into the wall reads:
'Thou who hast given me eyes to see,
And love this sight so fair,
Give me a heart to find out Thee,
And read Thee everywhere.'

These are the words of John Keble, Professor of Poetry at Oxford University between 1831 and 1841 as well as a highly respected churchman. But did he visit this spot? I doubt it, but perhaps he imagined a similar sight when he penned these words as he was writing about just how beautiful this world can be - and before your eyes is God's Country. Surprise View perhaps summarises the North York Moors better than any other single view as from this steep escarpment you can look out across Farndale and Douthwaite Dale, a valley of lush fields with the River Dove silently sparkling between trees and in the distance the brooding moors stretching away until they fade into the horizon. *This is the coloured corner of Yorkshire where the artist can be lavish with his palette. The roads are red, the bracken-covered slopes deep green or gold, according to the season, the miles of heather a sea of purple in autumn, and even the rocks and shales vary from bright red to a lustrous blue. The farmsteads and houses are colourful, too, and over all is the patina of a mellow age, for modernity has in general not entered here.* (**Harry Scott 'The English Counties' 1949**). Hidden amongst trees beside the River Dove in the beautiful valley of Douthwaite Dale, as the lower reaches of Farndale are known, stands Gillamoor Mill. There has been a mill on this site since at least the early 13th Century producing flour for over 700 years until it closed in 1895. It has since been restored and is now a private dwelling.

HUTTON-LE-HOLE is undeniably one of the prettiest villages in England, a jumble of quaint stone cottages set around an undulating village green cropped short by jaywalking sheep, through which flows Hutton Beck enclosed by white railings and spanned by numerous bridges; it is this picturesque green that gives the village its distinctive character. A scene reminiscent of the Cotswolds, but far superior as Hutton lies in a small wooded valley on the edge of the largest expanse of heather moorland in England, not to mention the fact that it is in Yorkshire! Hutton was named by Anglo-Saxon settlers who established a 'farm on a projecting ridge of land', although the suffix 'Hole' is a later addition and simply means 'in a hollow'; 'le' incidentally was added by the romantic Victorians. There have been people living in this area since prehistoric times as

Spaunton Moor to the north of the village is littered with prehistoric remains including burial mounds and field systems. Most of Hutton's houses date from between 1650 and 1750 when the old farms and cottages were rebuilt as prosperity increased. It was during this period that several Quaker families settled in the village in search of peace and quiet away from the persecution of their faith. Hutton's most famous Quaker was John Richardson, who came to live in the village in 1703 at what is now known as Quaker Cottage; the initials 'JR 1695' relate to his father-in-law John Robinson and not John Richardson as is often thought. Richardson won fame by travelling thousands of miles across America on horseback, not to mention many miles across England as well, spreading the word of George Fox, founder of the Quakers. Richardson was a friend of William Penn who fled to America where he established a Quaker colony which later became the state of Pennsylvania. Many of these Quakers were weavers producing woollen or linen products and soon a flourishing cottage industry became established. The village was also home to several miners who worked the small coal pits of Rudland Rigg and Blakey Ridge during the 18th Century, the coal being used mainly to fire the lime kilns. During the mid-19th Century when the ironstone mines of Rosedale began to be developed on a large scale the coal miners were replaced by ironstone miners who came to live in the village. Ironstone has been mined in this area since prehistoric times, indeed St Mary's Abbey at York held land around Hutton and Rosedale up until the Dissolution of the Monasteries producing iron-ore in small bloomeries. Next to The Crown is a house with an ornate inscription above the door that reads: 'By Hammer and Hand, All Arts do Stand" and the date 1784. This was originally the home of the village blacksmith, as this saying implies that all craftsmen were reliant on the skills of the blacksmith for their tools. The blacksmith was also an innkeeper and as the thirst of the miners' grew, the actual blacksmith's shop was rebuilt as a beerhouse in the 19th Century and was renamed The Crown.

In the heart of the village is the Ryedale Folk Museum, a fascinating open air museum set in three and a half acres of land with over fifteen historic buildings that have been carefully moved stone-by-stone to the museum. Of particular note is a heather-thatched cottage with a datestone of 1704 that was brought over from Stang End near Danby in 1967 and still retains its original witch post by the fire to ward off evil spirits; there are less than twenty witch posts still in existence, all of which can be found in North East Yorkshire apart from one in Lancashire. There is also a superb cruck-framed Elizabethan Manor House, a 16th Century glass furnace from Rosedale, a horse-drawn hearse that served the people of Farndale plus much more. It is almost a village in itself and provides a unique insight into everyday life for the people of the North York Moors in days gone by. A particularly fascinating corner is devoted to the many witches that once 'flew' around the more remote parts of the North York Moors; local people believed in witches, hob-goblins and fairies long after such superstition had died out elsewhere. A chilling reproduction of Peggy Duell's magic book, Hutton-le-Hole's very own witch, can still be seen in the Museum. A story is told of an old woman from Farndale who would turn herself into a black dog and terrify farmers as well as causing their animals to fall ill. One night a farmer lay in wait for this supernatural dog and when he saw it opened fire with his gun. The next day the farmer went round to see if this black dog was indeed the old woman as he suspected, and there she was lying in bed in agony suffering from gunshot wounds!

Common land in the area, which includes Hutton and Appleton Commons, Spaunton Moor and the village green, is still administered by the ancient Court Leet of the Manor of Spaunton, a relic of feudal times when the Court Leet was responsible for certain aspects of the law including minor offences, maintenance of commonland, grazing and turbary rights (peat cutting). This court dates back to Norman times, although it no longer deals with minor offences of the law, and consists of twelve jury members appointed by the Lord of the Manor who also presides over the Court. The Court meets once a year at the Manor House at Spaunton and its primary aim remains the management of the common, settlement of disputes and the protection of the rights and interests of commoners, an important role in medieval times and an early example of democracy. The Enclosure Acts of the late 18th and early 19th centuries saw the decline of these manor courts and only a handful remain today in England with four in the North York Moors. 'Fines' are still levied on people who encroach on the common land, which includes people's front gardens! Other buildings of note in the village includes the old pinfold near to the car park, a small stone circular enclosure where stray animals found on commonland were penned up and released after a fine was paid. The village school was built by public subscription in 1874 and once taught 80 children; however, it closed in 1972 and is now a gift shop. Hutton has always been part of the historic parish of Lastingham; however, a small Chapel-of-Ease was built in 1934, dedicated to St Chad, which now stands hidden amongst trees. All of this combines to make Hutton-le-Hole the most attractive village in the North York Moors, although Lealholm and Hawnby are strong contenders for the title. Through successful management of visitors, the scenes of cars parked across the green, litter and erosion are now thankfully confined to photographs of thirty years ago, but reputations are hard to change. Yes, there are one or two gift shops and the road through the village is often busy with cars heading over Blakey Ridge but when you arrive on foot late in the afternoon you will have the place almost to yourself, so spend some time exploring and you will be richly rewarded.

Hutton-le-Hole

STAGE TWO

. . . .

HUTTON-LE-HOLE
to
LEVISHAM

✦

*"In this world of clock-watching, stress and selfishness it often takes
something quite remarkable to make you stop and think. Something that
stands apart from the materialistic life many of us lead. Something that
touches upon the bigger picture. I made a point of looking into St Mary's
Church and apprehensively followed the narrow stone steps down from
the Nave into the crypt. My eyes took a second or two to adjust to the
light, although my skin and sense of smell were aroused by the damp,
cold atmosphere that hung heavy in the air. I walked towards the
apse with its small, single window throwing a shaft of light onto a
simple altar of rough stone. Unchanged for a thousand years, the
marks of the Norman stonemasons were as clear to see as when they
were made. The centuries somehow seemed to merge into a timeless
simplicity of thought and prayer, for people have come here to the
shrine of St Cedd for as long as there has been Christianity on
these shores. I am not a particularly religious person, but there is
something very spiritual about this crypt, a feeling that you are
surrounded by the prayers and faith of one and a half millennia.
All I know is that when I emerged into the outside world
I felt calm and at peace."*

Mark Reid
October 1999

WALK INFORMATION

Points of interest: Holy wells, step back 1,000 years into a unique Norman crypt, brewing barrels of beer, Roman training camps, a spectacular glacial gorge and the evocative sound of a steam train's whistle.

Distance:

Hutton-le-Hole to Cropton	5.5 miles
Cropton to Levisham	7.5 miles
Total	13 miles

Time: Allow 6 hours

Terrain: This walk follows clear paths across fields, through woodland and along enclosed 'green' lanes or quiet country roads. The sections between the River Seven and Cropton as well as the paths through woodland at the foot of Cawthorne Banks and Newton Banks can be muddy underfoot. The climb up Newton Banks is quite steep, although steps ease the ascent. The descent to Levisham Station and then up again to Levisham village is steep in places and care must be taken, particularly on the descent. Easy route-finding all the way.

Take care walking along the country lanes around Lastingham and Cropton. This walk includes two quite short but steep climbs as well as a steep descent. Many of the woodland paths are muddy underfoot. There is a small stream to cross in Raygate Slack.

Ascents:

Newton Banks:	195 metres
Levisham Station to village:	190 metres

Viewpoints: Extensive views across the North York Moors from the viewing platform at Cawthorn Roman Camps (slight detour from route).

Wonderful views of Newton Dale from the top of Newton Banks and Keldgate Slack.

FACILITIES

Hutton-le-Hole	Inn / B&B / Shop / Café / Bus / Phone / Toilets / Info
Lastingham	Inn / B&B / Bus / Phone
Cropton	Inn / B&B / Bus / Phone / Camp
Newton-on-Rawcliffe	Inn / B&B / Bus / Phone / Camp
Levisham Station	Café / Train / Toilets
Levisham	Inn / B&B / Phone

ROUTE DESCRIPTION

(Map Four)

Leave Hutton-le-Hole along the track to the right of the Ryedale Folk Museum (SP on railings 'Lastingham') passing between the houses and through the yard of The Barn Hotel then straight on across the gardens to reach a kissing-gate to the right of a wooden shed (thatched buildings of the Folk Museum on your left), after which carry straight on across the field (caravan site) alongside the hedge on your left (passing thatched buildings of Folk Museum on left) to reach a kissing-gate in the field corner (set in a belt of woodland). Head through the kissing-gate then walk straight on alongside the fence on your left for 100 yards and through an overgrown hedgerow where you head to the left (alongside this old hedgerow) to soon reach a gate in the field corner. After the gate, head straight on (fence on your left) to reach a FB across Fairy Call Beck (stream) that leads into woodland. Cross the FB then follow the clear path up through trees and on to join the road (SE 714 904). Turn right along the road for 0.5 miles then, just as the road curves to the right before the stone road-bridge, turn left along a track (SP) and through a gate. After the gate, follow the grassy track straight on then curving round to the right (heather moorland stretching away to your left), keeping close to the wall/fence on your right, then continue straight on along the bottom edge of the moorland for 0.25 miles heading towards Camomile Farm. As you approach Camomile Farm, the track forks - head straight on (waymarker-post) to soon reach the corner of the stone wall and stand of trees ahead of you, where you turn right down to a gate to the left of the buildings of Camomile Farm that leads onto a lane *(this short section from the corner of the wall to the gate is a permissive path across Open Access Land)*. Follow this lane down to reach the road which you follow to the left into Lastingham.

Follow the main road as it bends round to the left after the Blacksmith's Arms towards 'Cropton, Pickering, Rosedale' then round to the right then left again out of the village. Just before you leave the village take the FP to the right through a gate (SP) immediately after Gander Green House with its cattle grid (SE 731 903). Follow the path bending round to the right then straight on along the edge of the field down into woodland to reach a stone FB across Ings Beck, after which follow the woodland path (with Ings Beck to your left) up to reach a stile at the end of the woods. After the stile, head straight across the field (with Ings Beck across and down to your left) to reach a gate at the end of this field, after which continue straight on alongside the fence/Hagg Wood on your right for 0.5 miles to reach the road (Howldale Lane) through a gate (SE 739 896).

Turn left and follow the road down for approx. 0.25 miles then, just before the road-bridge across the River Seven (with the farm buildings of Lower Askew just beyond) take the FP to the right over a stile beside a gate (SP). After the stile, head straight on across two fields keeping close to the hedge on your left to reach a gate that leads into Scarth Wood. Follow the clear path through the woods *(steep drop down to the left)* to soon join a forest track, which you follow straight on then, where this track forks after a short distance, take the left-hand track that soon drops gently down into a slight dip, at the bottom of which follow the narrow path that branches off to the left (just as the track begins to rise up) heading straight on through the woods along the top of the steep bank (River Seven down to your left) to eventually re-join this track at the end of the woods. Turn left along this track and follow this straight on across two large fields, keeping to the perimeter of the field on your right, to reach a gate at Appleton Mill Farm. At the gate turn immediately left through a small gate *(do not enter farmyard)* and head alongside the fence/hedge *(same field as you have just been walking across)* to soon reach a large FB over the River Seven (SE 747 880). After the FB, head left through a gate then follow the grassy track up to soon join a clear track across your path where you turn left (SP 'Cropton'). Soon the track forks - follow the right-hand branch that leads uphill (track enclosed by mature trees) for 300 yards and through a gate, after which the track ends - carry straight on through the bridlegate ahead along the enclosed path (bridleway) and follow this overgrown path up to reach another bridlegate that leads onto an overgrown track (Bull Ing Lane) across your path (SE 753 881).

(Map Five)

Turn left here and follow the track (Bull Ing Lane) for 0.5 miles all the way to reach the road at Cropton (SE 755 888). Follow this road to the left into the village passing the New Inn on your left then, at the road junction, turn right towards 'Sutherland, Newton'. Follow the wide main road through the village, passing the old village well on your left then continue straight on along the road heading out of the village for 0.25 miles then, where the roads swings sharply round to the left, turn right (SP 'Cawthorne') along a stony lane (SE 759 895). Continue straight on along the stony lane passing Sycamore Farm on your right then Dalewood Farm on your left, after which the lane becomes a grassy track which you follow straight on (becomes quite overgrown) for 250 yards down to reach a bridlegate beside a field gate at the end of the track. After the gate, head diagonally to the left across the middle of the field towards the far left-hand corner to reach a stile in a fence that leads across a small enclosed field (caravan site) to join a track through woodland to quickly join the road (SE 767 896).

Turn right along the road (High Lane) then take the second turning on the left after 0.75 miles towards 'Keldy only' *(continue along road for 0.25 miles to reach entrance to Cawthorn Roman Camps)*. Follow the road straight on gently rising up for 0.25 miles to reach the crest of Cawthorne Banks where you carry on along the road down this bank, at the bottom of which take the BW to the right opposite Keldy Banks Farm (SP 'Bridleway'). Follow this clear path straight on through woodland along the edge of the woods on your right for 300 yards then follow the path as it meanders through the woods (birch trees) and down a sunken path to a FB across Cold Keld Beck. Cross the FB and follow the path as it bends to the left then gradually round to the right through woodland for 0.5 miles to eventually reach a metal gate at the end of the woods/heath (SE 785 913). Head straight on across the field to reach a gate to the right of High Cawthorn House that leads onto a metalled lane where you head straight on over this lane along the path directly ahead that immediately leads onto a grassy track. Follow this track straight on for almost 0.5 miles to join a clear stony track across your path on a bend (SE 786 921). Turn right here (waymarker-post) and follow this stony track (Peat Road) for 0.75 miles to reach a road (Stape Road).

(Map Six)

Head straight across the road along the FP opposite that leads through woodland (SP), keeping close to the perimeter on your left, to a stile at the end of the woods after which continue straight on across the large field alongside the hedge on your left to reach a stile in the corner of the field. Cross the stile and carry straight on through a small section of woodland to quickly join a clear farm track. Turn left along this track passing Upper Farm and continue on to quickly reach Middle Farm (SE 805 921). Immediately before the farm buildings of Middle Farm turn right along a path through undergrowth/woodland *(opposite the gate on the left)*. A clear path leads straight on for just over 0.5 miles through trees and then across heather/scrub moorland (Stony Moor) gradually dropping down into the wooded confines of Raygate Slack (valley), where you cross a stream to reach a bridlegate just beyond (SE 808 913). Head through the bridlegate and follow the wide path straight on up through woodland (stream and ravine of Raygate Slack down to your left) then bending round to the right climbing up Newton Banks (steps) all the way to the top of the bank. The track joins the road at the top of the village of Newton-on-Rawcliffe (SE 812 908); however, immediately before the road turn left along a stony track (SP 'Levisham'). After 125 yards views open out of Newton Dale; take the FP to the left over the stile at this point, after which turn right down a narrow path and continue straight on down hill *(ignore path that branches off to left near telegraph pole)*. The path soon swings left then slants steeply down the hillside to reach the bottom of the bank and a grassy track. Head straight on over the track heading towards Levisham Station (rooftops through trees) gently dropping down across the middle of the rough field (unclear path) to soon join a sunken path that leads steeply down through undergrowth/woodland to reach a FB over Pickering Beck and along a road to Levisham Station (SE 818 911).

Walk over the level crossing (station to your right) and head up the road across a cattle grid then take the path to the right immediately after the house on the right (SP 'Levisham') over a stream and through a gate into woodland. A clear path leads up through woods to reach a gate that brings you out on the open hillside then head straight uphill, bearing slightly to the right, to reach a stile next to a gate that leads onto a grassy track. Turn right along the track then almost immediately head up the wide, grassy path that branches up to the left slanting up the hillside (SP 'Village'). The path gradually climbs up across the hillside for 0.25 miles *(superb views across Newton Dale to your right)* then levels out (bench) and bends round to the left into a side-valley (Keldgate Slack). At the head of this side-valley turn right along a narrow path that traverses this valley up to a wall stile (SE 824 905). Cross the stile then turn left alongside the wall on your left across two large fields to join a road, which you follow straight on into Levisham.

The Blacksmiths Arms, Lastingham

MAP FOUR

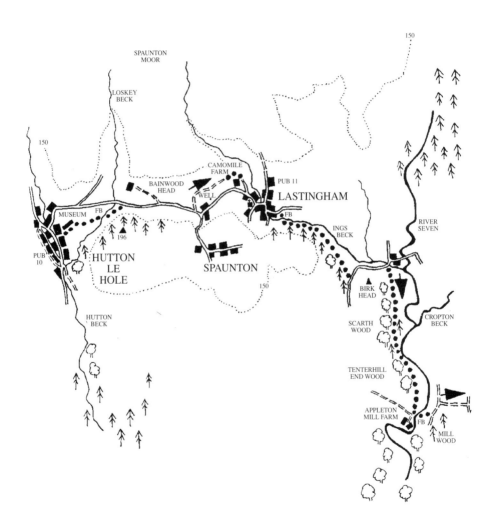

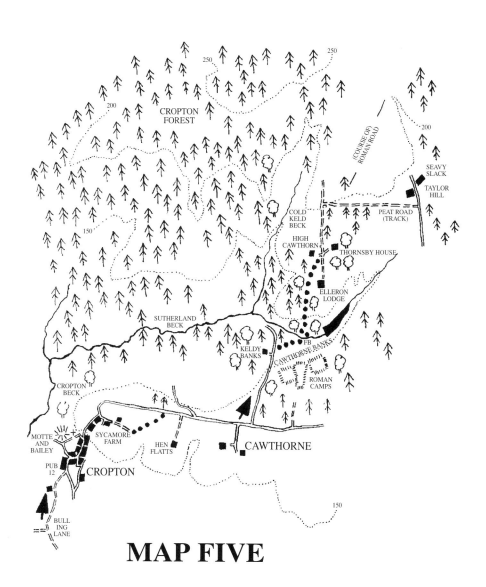

MAP FIVE

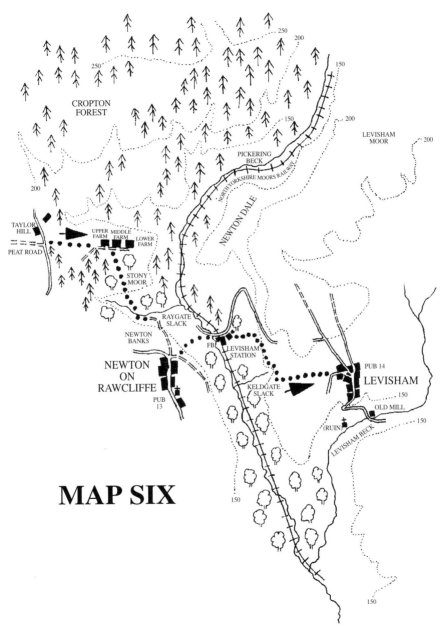

CROPTON
FOREST

250

200

150

250

200

150

PICKERING
BECK

LEVISHAM
MOOR

200

NORTH YORKSHIRE MOORS RAILWAY

NEWTON DALE

200

TAYLOR
HILL

UPPER MIDDLE
FARM FARM

LOWER
FARM

PEAT ROAD

STONY
MOOR

RAYGATE
SLACK

NEWTON
BANKS

FB

LEVISHAM
STATION

PUB 14

NEWTON
ON
RAWCLIFFE

KELDGATE
SLACK

LEVISHAM

PUB
13

150

OLD MILL

(RUIN)

150

LEVISHAM BECK

MAP SIX

150

150

LASTINGHAM shelters beneath the northerly escarpment of the Tabular Hills, a final oasis of sylvan beauty before a seemingly endless sea of lonely moorland that stretches away to the north. Tracks, well-worn with centuries of use, lead down from this moorland into the heart of the village through which flows Hole Beck, fed by a smaller roadside stream, both of which play a game of hide-and-seek beneath a succession of small bridges. Beside an overgrown pond near to Camomile Farm is a sad memorial to Ernest and Annie Parker, two small children who were playing on the grassy slope above the pond one day in May 1900 when they fell down the bank and drowned. It is a delight to walk through the village and admire the attractive assortment of immaculate cottages, a small green, old schoolhouse of 1885 that now serves as the village hall and a former Wesleyan Chapel complete with sundial. Lastingham is also famed for its three Holy Wells dedicated to St Cedd, St Chad and St Ovin, in remembrance of those early monks who brought the word of God here so many centuries ago. *"Aloof from the world in a green moorland hollow is this small place of great distinction and with an ancient tale to tell."* **(A. Mee 'Yorkshire North Riding' 1941)**. Attractive well-heads cover the springs that once provided the village with its water supply; the well dedicated to St Cedd still has a working tap. There is also a fourth Holy Well outside Lastingham to the east of a row of stone cottages near where the lane towards Hutton branches off to Spaunton. A trickle of crystal-clear water flows from this old wayside well, dedicated to Mary Magdalene, which lies hidden halfway down a small bank.

Tucked away in the heart of the village is the Blacksmith's Arms, a lovely old country inn that once had a very interesting landlady! Back in the 18th Century it was commonplace for absentee vicars to appoint a curate to look after their parish. Reverend Jeremiah Carter was one such curate who was paid an annual stipend of a piffling £20 with which he had to support his wife and thirteen children and so to make ends meet his wife ran the Blacksmith's Arms. To encourage people to attend the Sunday services, Jeremiah would often play his fiddle at the pub to the delight of the customers who would dance away the afternoon. However, the Archdeacon heard about this sacrilege and chastised poor Jeremiah, who pointed out that many of the parishioners had to travel long distances and would therefore seek refreshment at the pub before heading home. To keep them away from the evils of excessive drink and gossip he would entertain them by playing his fiddle: *"My parishioners enjoy a triple advantage, being instructed, fed and amused all at the same time. Moreover, this method of spending their Sunday is so congenial with their inclinations, that they are imperceptibly led along the paths of piety and morality..."* Jeremiah heard no more from the Archdeacon!

St Mary's Church dominates the village, one of the earliest sites of Christian worship in England for it was here in 654AD that St Cedd, a monk from Lindisfarne, established his Celtic monastery in what was then a remote and wild place. The Venerable Bede visited the monastery in the 8th Century and noted *"Cedd chose a site for the monastery among some high remote hills, which seemed more suitable for the dens of robbers and haunts of wild beasts than for human habitation."* Sadly St Cedd died of the plague in 664AD before his small wooden church had been completed; however, he was succeeded by his brother St Chad who proceeded to build a stone church over the tomb of St Cedd, who was buried next to the altar. Destroyed by invading Vikings in the 9th and 10th centuries, St Chad's monastery lay in ruins until the Norman Conquest, although the site was continually used for Christian worship. In 1078 Stephen, Abbot of Whitby, was granted permission by William the Conqueror to restore the monastery at Lastingham and so set about building a large stone church that was to form the heart of his new abbey. An ornate and spacious crypt was constructed where his body was thought to lie as a shrine to St Cedd. Above this crypt work began on the church itself; however, construction of this new church was abandoned in 1088 and the monks moved to St Mary's Abbey at York, probably due to roving bands of thieves coupled with its isolated location. They left behind a partly built abbey church that comprised of the apse, four pillars intended as supports for the central tower, foundations for the nave and the completed crypt. The abandoned abbey remained the property of St Mary's Abbey who provided a fulltime priest for the church in the 13th Century when they also consolidated the building to form the parish church we see today with the addition of a western wall, north and south aisles and arches between the tower pillars. The Norman crypt remains completely unaltered since the days of William the Conqueror and is unique as it has an apse, chancel, nave and aisles. It is a place of peace and serenity, with an overwhelming sense of spiritual well-being. The work of the Norman stonemasons can be clearly seen including ram's horn capitals on the supporting columns as well as numerous other ancient relics including Anglo-Saxon crosses, Viking tombstones, as well as carved stones and the actual altar from St Chad's original monastery. The church was restored twice during the 19th Century, initiated by John Jackson RA in 1828 due to the leaking roof, although his contribution was predominantly concerned with altering the church so that his painting of Correggio's 'The Agony in the Garden' could be displayed; a plaque outside Lidsty Cottage on the main street through the village identifies it as the birthplace of John Jackson RA. The church was more sympathetically restored in 1879 by J. L. Pearson, famed as the architect of Truro Cathedral, who designed the wonderful stone vaulted ceiling. *"...a wan light drifted over the hills and woods, and before I reached the humble village inn, thunder was crashing heavily around the hills, and the sky was torn right and left by branching antlers of forked lightning. The summer air darkened till all aspect of the day was gone; and in this spreading blackness, lit by the sudden lights that flashed from heaven, the strange old solitary life of monks among the dipping moorland hills became more real."* **(A. H. Norway 'Highways and Byways in Yorkshire' 1899).**

CROPTON lies just outside the National Park boundary, a strange omission considering its history and charm - surely a slip of the pen? Perhaps a blessing for Cropton remains unspoilt and is a delight to walk through; it is no surprise that it won the title of Best Kept Village North York Moors 1965. From the small green complete with old water pump sheltered by an ancient tree, the road curves through the village revealing a wide main street lined by attractive houses. Many of the houses were rebuilt during the 19th Century including a Methodist Chapel dated 1852 that is still in use, Reading Room of 1898, School of 1874 which is sadly decaying and the particularly attractive Morleys Terrace of 1877. A handful of older farms and cottages remain including Rose Cottage with its datestone of 1695 and inscription *'memento mori NC'*. Opposite this cottage is the old 300-ft village well that was capped in 1920, although the original winding gear and buckets can still be seen. This was once a thriving community that supported three pubs, now only the New Inn remains behind which stands Cropton Brewery, which produces an impressive range of award-winning real ales. For centuries Cropton was home to many quarrymen who worked the limestone quarries to the south of the village. The limestone was then fired in kilns to be used to 'sweeten' the more acidic soils of the central moors; the kilns were last fired in the 1960s.

A lane leads off the main street down to St Gregory's Church, a Victorian building on the site of a much older church as the old font testifies. In the churchyard are the remains of Cropton Cross, an ancient waymarker once used by travellers to guide them across the moors. As with many moorland crosses the tradition of placing coins or, in the case of the Cropton Cross, refreshment on top of the cross for less fortunate people has been practised for centuries and in some cases continues today. Such traditions may stem back to Roman times when offerings were made to gods to ensure a safe journey. Cropton Cross is also one of the few crosses to be featured in a rhyme: *"On Cropton Cross there is a cup, and in the cup there is a sup. Take that cup and drink that sup and put that cup on Cropton Cross."* Not the most imaginative rhyme in the world! In the field beyond the churchyard are the remains of Cropton Castle, an early 12th Century motte and bailey castle built by Robert de Stuteville consisting of a large earthen mound that would have been surmounted by a wooden palisade. This formed part of a string of Norman castles along the southern edge of the North York Moors including Thirsk, Helmsley, Pickering and Scarborough; however, Cropton Castle was not rebuilt in stone and fell into disuse as the neighbouring castles at Pickering and Helmsley were strengthened. The ramparts can still be seen including the impressive conical earthworks of the motte and ditches that are thought to have belonged to a manor hall, indeed the field is still known as Hall Garth.

Cropton's most famous son was Captain William Scoresby, renowned captain of whaling ships and Arctic explorer who was born in the village in 1760. Scoresby embarked on many journeys out of Whitby and became one of the most prolific whaling captains in Europe, introducing many revolutionary ideas to improve his whaling ships including the Crow's Nest which helped spot whales out at sea. In 1806 Scoresby navigated his ship to within a few hundred miles of the North Pole, closer than any person before him.

CAWTHORN ROMAN CAMPS are situated just off our route but are well worth the short diversion. Almost 2,000 years ago a contingent of soldiers left the Northern fortress of Eboracum (York) to consolidate this most northerly corner of the mighty Roman Empire and subdue the unruly Brigantes tribes who had previously ruled this land. They travelled north-eastwards by way of their fort at Derventio (Malton) and upon reaching the escarpment of the Tabular Hills set up a temporary marching camp at this strategic spot. This marching camp was subsequently consolidated with the addition of two forts and it is probable that this area was also used for military field training exercises. Abandoned in about 120AD when Hadrian's Wall was under construction, the ramparts lay undisturbed until they were excavated in the 1920s. However, recent excavations have shown that the site was used by Danish settlers around the 9th Century as the remains of a small group of buildings built from turf and thatch have been uncovered. These Roman remains are unique as they comprise a series of three Roman camps, originally believed to have been Practice Camps where Roman soldiers came to perfect their fort building techniques, but it is now known to consist of two occupied forts with a central marching camp. Many questions still remain unanswered, and we can only speculate as to why they were built and who was garrisoned here. It is a fascinating place to explore along a way-marked one mile route, with the ramparts of the two forts with their classic playing-card shape clearly visible flanking a central oblong marching camp; the western fort is particularly well defended with double ditches and deep earthen banks. The forts were built right on the edge of the escarpment from where there are breathtaking views across the vast Cropton Forest. At the end of the first Century AD a Roman infantry soldier would no doubt have stood on duty at this very spot looking out across the moors, dreaming of home far away.

NEWTON-UPON-RAWCLIFFE was first settled by an Anglo-Saxon farmer who built his 'new farm' on this gently sloping shelf of fertile land. Newton has developed into a peaceful village with an assortment of attractive cottages and farms set around a spacious village green at the heart of which is a pond complete with noisy ducks. *"At the village of Newton, perched on high ground far above the dale, we come to the limit of civilisation. The sun is nearly setting. The cottages are scattered along the wide roadway and the strip of grass, broken by two large ponds, which just now reflect the pale evening sky. Straight in front, across the green, some ancient barns are thrown up against the golden sunset, and the long perspective of white road, the geese, and some whitewashed gables, stand out from the deepening tones of the grass and trees."* **(G. Home 'Yorkshire' 1908).** Newton's pond is one of the few surviving village ponds left in this part of the North York Moors as at one time most villages of the Tabular Hills would have had a clay-lined pond, a necessity due to the underlying pervious limestone rock strata. Adjacent to the Methodist Chapel at the foot of the village is a pinfold, which was used up until the late 19th Century. This small stone enclosure was used by the Pindar to impound stray animals. Across the road stands St John's Church, built in 1868 to replace the 16th Century Chapel-of Ease that once stood at the top of village next to Quern House. The church is well worth exploring as it boasts a particularly fine high-pitched roof, 'Mousey' Thompson furniture and, most interestingly of all, the intricate cogs and weights of the church's bell and clock mechanism on display for all to see.

Our route follows the track from the top of the village to the edge of Newton Banks where a spectacular view suddenly unfolds. This view of the deep wooded gorge of Newton Dale never fails to thrill and excite with the sinuous track-bed of the North Yorkshire Moors Railway threading its way along the gently curving valley floor. It is quite a surprise to find such a dramatic valley in the North York Moors, but this area is full of surprises, as you will discover. Many people believe the North York Moors to be drab moorland that you drive across to get to the coast, but that is because the secrets of the Moors do not reveal themselves to the car-bound - you have to get out and walk! Newton Dale Gorge was scoured out during the last Ice Age over 10,000 years ago by powerful glacial meltwaters that thundered down this channel after overflowing from a huge glacial lake that filled the Esk Valley; this is the finest example of a glacial overflow channel in England. A bench offers a welcome opportunity to rest weary legs and admire the view, but pause for a while for this bench stands as a memorial to Kenneth and Patrick Evans who 'enjoyed the freedom of the moors' as boys but were both tragically killed at the young age of 21 during the Second World War. We are fortunate to be able to sit and admire the view whilst others dreamt of such a spot when surrounded by the horrors of war.

THE NORTH YORKSHIRE MOORS RAILWAY offers a glimpse of the 'golden age of steam' with beautifully preserved stations, signal boxes, carriages and locomotives. This historic line runs for 18 miles from Pickering through the very heart of the North York Moors National Park until it joins the Esk Valley line at Grosmont, a scenic journey of pure delight through remote countryside. From Pickering the line gradually climbs along the floor of the Newton Dale Gorge, then crosses desolate Fen Bogs, a Nature Reserve of wetland peat bog up to 40-ft deep, before reaching Goathland from where the line drops down into the confines of the Murk Esk valley, with waterfalls and wooded ravines flashing past the window all the way to Grosmont. *"It is a question whether there is quite such another railway line as this in England. It winds in and out between high hills; beneath overhanging woods; alongside brawling streams; across* *hillside rivulets, rushing to meet them; past houses perched hundreds of feet above the valley through which the train twists its way like a snake; now past a quiet village, and now past a smelting mine, until at last it runs into the valley of the Esk."* (**J. S. Fletcher 'The Enchanting North' 1908**).

The railway was completed in 1836 and originally only connected Pickering with Whitby to provide a stimulus for its flagging whaling and shipbuilding industries. Designed by George Stephenson, the 'Father of the Railways', this was one of the first passenger railways in the world, although the carriages were initially horse-drawn. The obstacle of the steep incline at Beck Hole, which featured a gradient of 1-in-10, was overcome by a complex system of ropes, pulleys and water-tanks that hauled the carriages up the slope, whilst at Fen Bogs whole trees, heather bales bound with sheepskins and moss-covered hurdles were sunk into the peat bog to provide a foundation. George Hudson, the 'Railway King' bought the line in 1845 and set about upgrading it for locomotive use. He built new bridges, tunnels, stations and connected the railway with the main Scarborough to York line. However, the famous Beck Hole 'incline' was only bypassed in 1865 when the 'Deviation Route' was blasted out between Grosmont and Moorgates near Goathland reducing the incline to a gradient of 1-in-49, an amazing feat of Victorian engineering. Following the Beeching Report, the section between Grosmont and Pickering was controversially closed in 1965, although the Esk Valley line from Middlesbrough to Whitby remained open thanks to concerted local campaigning. The North Yorkshire Moors Railway Preservation Society was formed in 1967 and subsequently bought back the line from British Railways, re-opening it fully to the public in 1973 as a preserved steam railway, run by very professional enthusiasts who operate regular services from April until November between Pickering and Grosmont. In 2007 the North Yorkshire Moors Railway secured agreement from Network Rail to operate steam trains between Grosmont and Whitby, thus re-establishing steam trains along the entire length of this historic railway between Whitby and Pickering.

LEVISHAM STATION lies hidden away in Newton Dale, over a mile and a rather stiff climb from the village it was built to serve but, as the local joke goes, the reason why the station is so far from the village is that they wanted it to be next to the railway line! For me, this is one of the finest spots in the North York Moors, and you can not help but peer down the tracks in case there is a train coming. Excitement fills the air as the screech of the engine's whistle echoes down the valley and intensifies as the engine comes into sight with steam hissing from pistons, billowing grey smoke chuffing out of the funnel and half a dozen carriages rattling along the tracks behind. The station is a wonderful place, with such incredible attention to detail that you feel as though you have stepped back in time with a level crossing, old-fashioned signal box that also doubles as a ticket office, waiting rooms and sidings with old rolling stock; the stone-built Station House and cottages dates from Stephenson's original line of 1836. It is no wonder that such an unspoilt location has been used in many television programmes including Heartbeat, All Creatures Great and Small and Brideshead Revisited.

Levisham Station

LEVISHAM lies on the southern edge of a gently rising shelf of land, with the plunging ravines of Newton Dale and Levisham Beck to the east, west and south; Levisham feels like an island 'cut off' from the rest of the world. It was a Saxon farmer called Leofgeat who first built his farm here over a thousand years ago, since when Levisham has matured into a refined village of mellow stone houses and farms facing across a well-kept green, complete with maypole, that runs the entire length of the village. Levisham's pond was situated between the church and the pub; however, it was filled in many years ago. There are still four working farms in the village whilst the tiny Post Office opens for two mornings a week *(sadly, the Post Office closed in 2004)*.

Levisham's Church, dedicated to St John the Baptist, was a Chapel-of-Ease until the 1950s when the much older Parish Church of St Mary, which is situated in the deep valley between Levisham and Lockton, fell into disuse. In the porch of this former Chapel-of-Ease is an Anglo-Danish gravestone with a rare and intricate carved dragon whilst inside the church is a Norman font, both of which came from the older church; note the list of Rectors, an unbroken succession since July 1289. The sad ruins of St Mary's Church are worth the short walk from the village down the steep, winding road towards Lockton. A place of worship since at least the 11th Century, the crumbling tower and roofless remains have a sad and melancholy atmosphere in contrast with the peaceful surroundings. The reason why St Mary's was built in such a secluded spot is uncertain; perhaps it was because the church served both Levisham and Lockton or possibly this was the site of a medieval settlement that later moved to higher ground in an attempt to prevent the spread of the Great Plague which they thought to be water-borne. *"...the villages of Lockton and Levisham face each other across a deep ravine. Levisham's old church stands at the bottom between them, but these Anglian and Danish settlements cherished for centuries a fierce antagonism, and even to-day have little combined life."* **(E. Pontefract and M. Hartley 'Yorkshire Tour' 1939)**. Near the church along the road stands Levisham Mill, complete with rusting waterwheel.

STAGE THREE

. . . .

LEVISHAM
to
EGTON BRIDGE

✦

*"Often overlooked, perhaps even berated by some historians as a haven
for rowdy drunks and social misfits, the British pub deserves more
recognition for they are an integral part of our heritage and form the
cultural bedrock of our society. For 2,000 years these uniquely British
institutions have witnessed many of our defining historical moments; they
are interwoven with the history of this country. From the very first
Roman 'Tabernae', to monastic hospices, coaching inns and Victorian
public houses, the development of our pubs has continued through the
ages and where better is there to experience this rich culture than in a
welcoming country inn? So, blow off the froth and imbibe heartily
of our heritage gulp by gulp before 'theme' bars sweep the land...
Tucked away in the small village of Beck Hole stands one of the finest
country pubs in England. It is small, old fashioned, unpretentious, yet
there is something very special about this pub. During the 19th Century
when the local ironstone mines flourished the Birch Hall Inn became a
full-time pub and village shop, a tradition that still continues to this day.
The pub is divided into three rooms with a small shop sandwiched
between the even smaller bar and lounge; it is an absolute gem that
mere words can not do justice – go and visit it, buy yourself a pint,
soak up the atmosphere and help ensure our heritage is passed on
to the next generation in good working order."*

Mark Reid
December 1999

WALK INFORMATION

Points of interest: Precipitous cliffs and breath-taking views, expansive heather moorland, Bronze Age burial mounds, a famous TV policeman, the ancient game of quoits, a classic country pub and the village missed by the Reformation.

Distance:

Levisham to Goathland		10 miles
Goathland to Egton Bridge		5 miles
Total		15 miles

Time: Allow 7 hours

Terrain: Clear moorland tracks lead across Levisham Moor to reach Skelton Tower from where a clear path follows the top of the escarpment above Newton Dale (sheer cliffs in places) before a narrow path leads steeply down into the side valley of Havern Beck to reach the railway line through Newton Dale. There is then a steep climb up through dense forest onto Killing Nab Scar (north side of Newton Dale) from where a clear path leads through forest along the top of the escarpment (sheer cliffs) to join a forest track. Forest tracks then lead through Cropton Forest to reach Wardle Green from where a clear path (muddy underfoot and exposed to the elements) heads across the open moorland of Two Howes Rigg to Goathland. The section from Goathland to Egton Bridge follows clear paths across pastures, through woodland and along part of the Rail Trail (route of Stephenson's original 1836 railway between Grosmont and Goathland), with a short but steep climb out of Darnholme. *The path along the top of Huggitt's Scar, Yewtree Scar and Killing Nab Scar runs along the top of the escarpment above Newton Dale with steep drops and sheer rock faces in places, although there is flat moorland or forest on the opposing side. The path that descends alongside Havern Beck is narrow and steep, with steep drops to the side of the path. Take care crossing the railway line through Newton Dale, as well as the minor roads between Goathland and Egton Bridge. Route finding may be difficult in mist across Two Howes Rigg.*

Open Access	The section from Levisham Bottoms to Hudson's Cross and then from Needle Point to the Forest Drive (Cropton Forest) heads across Open Access land **www.openaccess.gov.uk**
Ascents:	Killing Nab Scar: 230 metres Simon Howe: 260 metres
Viewpoints:	Skelton Tower, Yewtree Scar, Needle Point and Killing Nab Scar offer superb views across Newton Dale. The hills above Darnholme offer good views across the valleys of Eller Beck and West Beck. The final descent into Egton Bridge affords views along the length of Esk Dale towards Whitby with the North Sea clearly visible on the horizon.

FACILITIES

· ·

Levisham	Inn / B&B / Phone
Goathland	Inn / B&B / Shop / Café / Bus / Train / Phone / Toilets / Camp
Beck Hole	Inn / B&B / Shop
Egton Bridge	Inn / B&B / Bus / Train / Phone / Toilets

ROUTE DESCRIPTION

Leave Levisham along the road that passes to the left of the Horseshoe Inn towards 'Levisham Station'. Follow the road for almost 0.5 miles then, where it turns sharp left towards 'Levisham Station', continue straight on along the lane (Braygate Lane). Follow this lane straight on for 0.5 miles (lane becomes a rough track) to reach a gate at the end of the enclosed track, with the open moorland of Levisham Moor ahead (SP 'Goathland'). Head through the gate and follow the grassy track straight on across heather moorland keeping close to the stone wall on your left (SP 'Bridleway') then, where this wall bends away to the left after 0.3 miles, continue straight on along this track over open moorland to reach the crest of a steep bank (West Side Brow). A clear track slants down this bank to the right then levels out and heads across a shelf of moorland to reach Skelton Tower (ruin) overlooking Newton Dale (SE 820 929).

As you reach Skelton Tower, turn right along a grassy path that follows the edge of the escarpment (with Newton Dale down to your left) sweeping round to the left. The path soon joins a clear but rough grassy track, which you follow straight on across the fairly narrow shelf of undulating land (Levisham Bottoms) with the escarpment above Newton Dale to your left and the steep bank of West Side Brow to your right. After 0.75 miles the track passes through a narrow section enclosed by West Side Brow on your right and the escarpment on your left then, where this shelf of land opens out, take the FP to the left (waymarker-post) - do not continue along the track ahead. *Take care along this next section; do not venture too close to the edge.* Follow this narrow path through heather/bracken along the top of the escarpment (with Newton Dale falling away to your left) for 1 mile passing along the top of Huggitt's Scar (with Kidstye Farm down to your left in the bottom of the valley) to eventually reach Hudson's Cross with its trickling waterfall (steep side-valley that feeds into Newton Dale - SE 839 946). Follow the path skirting around the top of Hudson's Cross *(ignore FP down to Newtondale Halt)* then continue along the FP that follows the top of the escarpment across Yewtree Scar *(caution: sheer cliffs)* for 0.5 miles until you reach a wall/fence across your path. At the wall turn right and head alongside the wall then, where this wall bends away to the left, head straight on bearing very slightly to the left to quickly reach a kissing-gate in a fence, overlooking the deep side-valley of Havern Beck (SE 846 948). Head through the kissing-gate and follow the path straight on, with Havern Beck falling steeply away to your right - the path is level at first but soon heads quite steeply down *(caution: steep drops to the side of the path)* into the ravine of Havern Beck. The path eventually reaches the valley floor and follows Havern Beck for a short distance, then crosses a FB over the stream and heads across boggy ground to reach the railway line along the flat valley floor of Newton Dale (SE 844 954).

Cross the railway line *(take care)* and follow the path up to join a forestry track. Turn left along this track and follow it as it soon bends round to the right then, just before it begins to bend round to the left, take the FP to the right (waymarker-post) that leads steeply up steps through the forest (SE 843 952). Head up the clear path all the way up through the forest to the top of the escarpment, where you turn left (waymarker-post) along the top of the escarpment heading through woodland to soon reach the promontory of Needle Point (SE 842 953). As you reach Needle Point, follow the path to the right heading along the top of the escarpment (Newton Dale down to your left) for 0.2 miles then round to the left again to run along the top of Killing Nab Scar (escarpment) for just over 0.5 miles to eventually reach a clear forest track at the head of the stream of Yaul Sike Slack (SE 832 954). Turn left along this track *(ignore FP off to the left after a short distance)* and follow it for approx. 0.3 miles to reach the wide Forest Drive road at a crossroads of tracks and roads (SE 827 952). *This section of path from Needle Point to the Forest Drive road is not a Right of Way; however, it follows a permissive path courtesy of the Forestry Commission who allow free public access through Cropton Forest. Please observe any 'Forest Operations' warning signs. Take care when walking along the top of Killing Nab Scar*. Turn right along the Forest Drive and follow this straight on then take the third track on the right (barrier with blue waymarker) where the forest opens out into fields on your right (SE 821 953). Follow this grassy track straight on for 0.25 miles, with forest on your right and hedge/fields on your left, to reach a clearer track across your path. Head straight on over this track through a gate opposite then bear to the right across the middle of the field to a small gate in a fence. Continue straight on with the fence/forest on your right then, where this forest ends, carry on down to quickly reach a gate in a fence across your path, after which continue straight on along the clear path heading gently down the hillside, over a stony track and carry straight on down (plantation on your right) to a small gate to the right of a ruined stone building at Wardle Green (with the open moorland of Simon Howe Rigg ahead - SE 824 963).

(Map Eight)

Head through the gate, over a FB then follow the path climbing gradually up across heather moorland passing to the left of a semi-circular stone enclosure, after which the path bends slightly to the right and heads up across the gently rising wide ridge (Simon Howe Rigg) for 1 mile to reach the prominent landmark of Simon Howe *(Bronze Age burial mound)*. As you approach Simon Howe, follow the path skirting to the left of Simon Howe and its small hill *(the path up to the cairn is not a Right of Way, although this moorland is Open Access land)* and soon joins the clearer path again after Simon Howe. Continue along this path heading straight on. The path soon divides (SP), follow the left-hand branch that gradually sweeps round to the left for 0.75 miles to reach the prominent mounds of Two Howes (SE 825 994). As you approach the left-hand mound of Two Howes *(Bronze Age burial mounds)* the path forks, follow the right-hand path up to quickly reach the left-hand of the two burial mounds with its large cairn. As you reach this cairn, follow the clear path to the left heading down across the moorland then gently curving round to the right for 0.5 miles down to reach The Tarn (small lake). As you reach

The Tarn, follow the path to the right passing The Tarn on your left, just after which follow the grassy path curving to the left up a small bank. At the top of this small bank, carry straight on across the grassy moorland gently dropping down for 0.25 miles to reach a bench where you follow the path heading steadily down to the right towards Goathland to reach the road junction near to the church (NZ 826 006).

Head along the road through the village (road-sign 'Whitby 9') passing the church on your right, then the row of shops and continue down along the road to eventually reach Goathland Station (North Yorkshire Moors Railway) at the bottom end of the village (0.75 miles from the church). At the Station, cross the railway lines and head through the old metal gate opposite *(use footbridge if train in station)*, after which turn immediately left (SP 'Darnholme') and head up alongside the fence/wall on your left (railway down to your left), over the hill then steeply down towards Darnholme set in a small valley. The path crosses the large FB to the left (over Eller Beck) just before you reach the ford and quickly heads up to join the road, where you turn right to cross the ford/stepping stones back over Eller Beck (NZ 835 022). After the ford, follow the track straight on then, where the track bends to the right after a short distance, take the FP branching off to the left that quickly leads over a FB across a stream, after which follow the clear path straight on winding steeply up across the hillside to the top of the bank. At the top of the bank, follow the path straight on alongside the stone wall on your left to soon reach a gate on your left, where the wall ends and a fence begins. Turn left over a stile by this gate and follow the clear path straight on, which soon becomes a track that leads behind a house. As you reach the back of the house, carry straight on along the grassy path ahead alongside the wall on your right to soon reach a small gate that leads out onto the open hillside. After the gate, carry straight on along the grassy path alongside the wall on your right *(heading across the top of the bank, with the valley of Eller Beck falling away to your left)* to soon reach a fork in the path where you follow the right-hand path heading alongside the wall on your right to soon reach another fork in the path (waymarker-post) where you branch off to the left along a narrow path through bracken slanting gradually down across the hillside to soon reach a crossroads of paths just before a stone enclosure (with its large tree and three smaller ash trees - NZ 829 024). Turn left here and drop down across the hillside to reach a railway bridge above Eller Beck *(do not cross FB)* where you turn right along the fence heading across the side of the hill, with Eller Beck down to your left, to reach a bench above the railway viaduct. As you reach this bench, bear slightly right heading straight on alongside the wall/fence on your left to join a grassy farm track that leads on to join a metalled farm lane beside Hill Farm (NZ 823 024). Turn left along this lane down to reach the road, where you turn left over the railway bridge and steeply down into Beck Hole.

(Map Nine)

Follow the road through the village, over the bridge and past the Birch Hall Inn, immediately after which take the track to the right (SP 'Bridleway') that leads down through gates and onto the old track-bed of Stephenson's original railway (NZ 821 021). Turn right (SP 'Grosmont'), over a FB across the Murk Esk (river) passing the site of the former station and continue along the old cinder track-bed, over another small bridge then, before the next large bridge, turn right (SP 'Grosmont, Rail Trail') then left over a stile by a gate. A clear path now heads through woodland alongside the Murk Esk to join the old track-bed again near to a new FB across the Murk Esk river. Do not cross this FB but continue along the old railway line through woodland (river on your left) for approx. 0.25 miles to reach a bridlegate at the end of the woods. Head through the bridlegate and continue straight on along the raised track-bed across fields to reach the next FB across the Murk Esk, approx. 100 yards after which turn left off this track over a stile by a gate (NZ 820 036). After the gate, head straight up the hillside along the indistinct grassy track alongside the fence on your right then, as the track bears away to the left, continue up across the hillside alongside the fence on your right to reach a gate that leads into woodland (Spring Wood). Follow the stony path up and round to the left through Spring Wood to a gate at the end of the woods, after which continue climbing up along the grassy track keeping to the perimeter of the field on your left to reach a gate that leads onto the farm track just to the right of Dowson Garth Farm. Cross the track and head through the gate opposite, after which follow the path up to the left alongside the fence on your left to reach a wall-stile in the field corner, after which carry straight on through a belt of woodland that leads onto the road to the left of High Burrows Farm (NZ 813 040).

Cross the road and head along the FP through the gate opposite, past a barn and head straight on across the field keeping close to the wall/hedge on your right to reach a gateway to the right just before the end of the field, after which turn left alongside the wall on your left to reach a wall-stile at the end of the field. Cross the stile and bear right across the field to reach the corner of a wood where you turn right, now with the wood on your left, over a stile and down the hillside alongside the wall to a gate in the bottom left corner of the field. Head left through this gate then walk straight on across fields, keeping to the wall on your right, and through a gate immediately to the left of the stone barn (Low Hollins Farm) that leads onto a farm track, which you follow down to reach the road (NZ 806 045). At the road, turn right to soon reach a road turning to the right - take the FP straight on through the farmyard of Blue Beck Cottage and through a gate to the left of the house. Head down the hillside keeping the fence on your left to a stile that leads into woodland. Follow the path to the left, keeping to the top of the bank, through the woods then straight on across the top of a field to reach a stile that leads back into woodland. A clear path drops down through the woods to join a track, which you follow to the left to join the main road through Egton Bridge *(turn left along the road for the Horseshoe Hotel or right for the Postgate Inn and train station).*

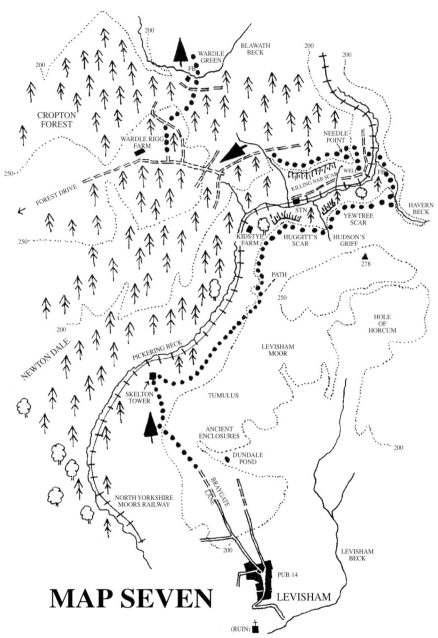

MAP SEVEN

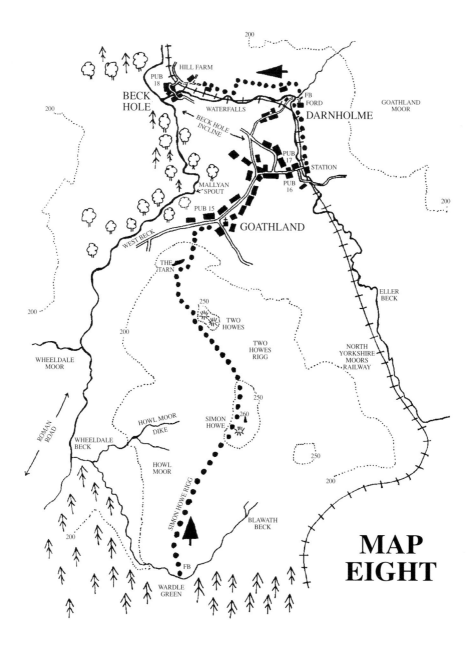

HILL FARM

PUB 18

BECK HOLE

200

WATERFALLS

FB
FORD

DARNHOLME

GOATHLAND MOOR

BECK HOLE INCLINE

PUB 17

STATION

MALLYAN SPOUT

PUB 16

PUB 15

GOATHLAND

WEST BECK

200

THE TARN

ELLER BECK

250

TWO HOWES

200

TWO HOWES RIGG

NORTH YORKSHIRE MOORS RAILWAY

200

WHEELDALE MOOR

250

ROMAN ROAD

HOWL MOOR DIKE

SIMON HOWE

260

250

WHEELDALE BECK

HOWL MOOR

SIMON HOWE RIGG

200

BLAWATH BECK

200

MAP EIGHT

FB

WARDLE GREEN

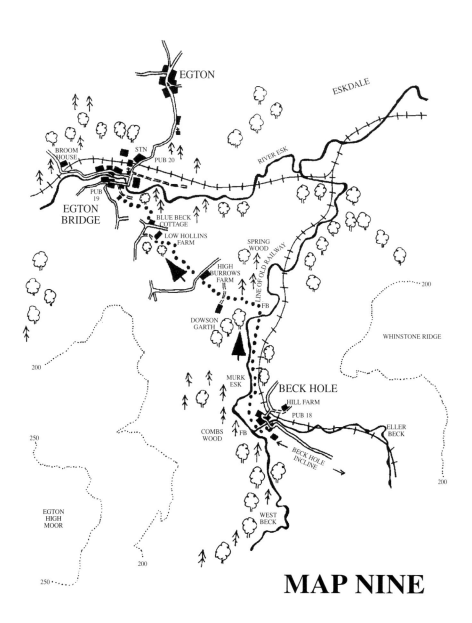

EGTON

ESKDALE

BROOM HOUSE

STN

PUB 20

RIVER ESK

PUB 19

EGTON BRIDGE

BLUE BECK COTTAGE

LOW HOLLINS FARM

SPRING WOOD

LINE OF OLD RAILWAY

HIGH BURROWS FARM

FB

200

DOWSON GARTH

WHINSTONE RIDGE

200

MURK ESK

BECK HOLE

HILL FARM

PUB 18

250

COMBS WOOD

FB

ELLER BECK

BECK HOLE INCLINE

200

EGTON HIGH MOOR

WEST BECK

200

250

MAP NINE

LEVISHAM MOOR stretches for several miles to the north of the village, a beautiful swathe of heather moorland that forms part of the 3,350-acre Levisham Estate, owned and managed by the North York Moors National Park Authority who purchased this land in 1976 to safeguard the area from changing farming methods and the spread of bracken that threatened the traditional heather moorland. Levisham Moor is littered with important archaeological sites including Bronze Age burial mounds and Iron Age settlements, enclosures, dykes and even the site of a rare bloomery, or iron smelting furnace. The area also offers open access for walkers who come to appreciate the purple moors of late summer, ancient woodland, cliffs of Newton Dale and the famous Hole of Horcum. This immense natural amphitheatre was formed, according to local folklore, by a giant called Wade who scooped out the earth whilst in one of his many rages and threw it at his wife Bell. He was not a good shot by all accounts and the large handful of earth whistled past his wife's head and landed over a mile away to the east to form the small rounded hill of Blakey Topping. A more mundane explanation is that the Hole of Horcum is the result of the erosive action of springs over thousands of years, known as spring-sapping, and not glacial meltwater as is often cited.

SKELTON TOWER stands sentinel above the spectacular Newton Dale Gorge. This small stone structure was built in 1850 by Robert Skelton, Rector of Levisham, who was a rather eccentric character by all accounts. It was built as a folly, not as a shooting lodge as many people believe, where the Rev. Skelton could escape from the tumult of the world to clear his mind, write sermons, gaze across the beauty of Newton Dale down towards the railway line and enjoy a quiet drink! The roofless remains of Skelton Tower look forlornly out across an unchanged scene that still provokes a sense of calm and inner thought; it is an inspirational place.

Skelton Tower

NEWTON DALE GORGE is the finest example of a glacial meltwater channel in this country, scoured out over 10,000 years ago by great torrents of water thundering down this once small valley. At the close of the last Ice Age the North York Moors was a vast area of tundra surrounded by glaciers with the huge Scandinavian Glacier in the North Sea and smaller glaciers from the British Ice Caps in the Vale of York. As the ice began to retreat, meltwater became trapped behind moraines and ice sheets creating lakes which then backed up and overflowed, however this meltwater was prevented from following the natural drainage pattern by the surrounding glaciers so the only way this water could go was south across the heart of the North York Moors. The Esk Dale lake stretched for over eleven miles making it even bigger than Windermere, England's largest lake, and spilled over into Glaisdale and the Murk Esk Valley from where it poured over Fen Bogs and down Newton Dale to create another huge lake in the Vale of Pickering; in a matter of a few decades Newton Dale Gorge had been created. Newton Dale stretches for over ten miles from Pickering to Fen Bogs, a precipitous gorge for most of its length with sheer cliffs and steep wooded slopes rising up to 400 feet above the valley floor; this is Yorkshire's 'Grand Canyon'. Our walk follows the dramatic cliff edge for most of the way along Huggitt's Scar and Yewtree Scar then down into the ravine of Havern Beck; this is walking country par excellence with heather moorland to your right covering the flat shelf of land known as Levisham Bottoms and incredible cliffs that certainly gets the adrenaline flowing! *"...I was on the brow of what could only by the grossest flattery be called a ravine. It was an abyss, and the road ran straight down by a gradient which was even as the gradient of a teacup. Down below me, in the very bowels of the earth, was a pretty valley, winding among the steep shags of gorse and ling that dropped precipitously to it on every side."* **(A. H. Norway 'Highways and Byways in Yorkshire' 1899)**.

KILLING NAB SCAR, sometimes referred to as Killingnoble Scar, offers perhaps the finest view of Newton Dale Gorge either from the scar itself or from the promontory of Needle Point. This whole area from Pickering to Goathland was a Royal hunting preserve dating back to Norman times, known as the Forest of Pickering and administered from Pickering Castle; indeed much of this area remains the property of the reigning Sovereign through the Duchy of Lancaster. In medieval times peregrine falcons nested on Killing Nab Scar and were used by the King for hunting; the villagers of Goathland were charged with looking after these valuable birds. *"The rocks are at their finest at Killingnoble Scar, where they take the form of a semicircle on the west side of the railway. The scar was for a very long period famous for the breed of hawks, which were specially watched by the Goathland men for the use of James I; and the hawks were not displaced from their eyrie even by the incursion of the railway into the glen, and only recently became extinct."* **(G. Home 'Yorkshire' 1908)**.

Under this scar is Newton Dale Well, a spring that flows over a tiered cistern and turns the rocks a brilliant orange colour. This well has been used by people since prehistoric times when such a spring rising straight out of rock would have caused wonderment, the only explanation would have been the work of some kind of god or mystical power. In the 17th Century a small well house was built to enable visitors to bathe in the waters and in 1734 Dr Short recommended the healing powers of the water to restore weakened limbs and joints in his book 'History of the Mineral Waters'. Interestingly, Dr Short was also instrumental in bringing the mineral waters of Harrogate to the public's attention and so helped establish the world's first Spa Town. By the early 19th Century the Well had fallen into disuse and had become overgrown, however the arrival of the railway brought new hope and plans were drawn up in 1893 to create a Spa and railway station; thankfully the plans did not materialise.

CROPTON FOREST is one of the largest forests in the country which, along with neighbouring Dalby Forest to the east as well as many other smaller forests, forms part of the vast North York Moors Forest District that covers some 23,000 hectares, all of which is managed by the Forestry Commission. Following the First World War there was great concern about the state of Britain's resources as timber supplies had almost been exhausted. In response to this the Forestry Commission was established to provide the country with timber and soon large areas of marginal moorland and mountain were planted with trees. Cropton Forest was first planted during the 1920s using only a handful of coniferous tree species, a policy that became heavily criticised. In recent years much more attention has been given to the natural contours of the land and over a dozen varieties of coniferous and nearly as many deciduous species are now planted to give a less uniform appearance, although Sitka Spruce and Scots Pine still dominate. The forests have been opened up for recreational purposes, particularly Dalby Forest which is known as the 'Great Yorkshire Forest' with a Visitor Centre at Low Dalby, waymarked paths, bridleways and the popular Dalby Forest Drive. These forests also provide hundreds of full time and seasonal jobs, a real boost for the local rural economy. Cropton Forest is a valuable refuge for a variety of wildlife including deer, fox, badger, squirrel, bat, owl, sparrowhawk as well as many other woodland birds.

TWO HOWES RIGG is an expanse of open heather moorland that gradually rises from the outskirts of Goathland to a height of 252 metres above sea level at Two Howes and 260 metres at Simon Howe further to the south. 'Howe' is the Old Norse word for a burial mound, indeed the North York Moors are littered with thousands of Bronze Age burial sites, or tumuli, offering a unique insight into these often misunderstood people. These tumuli form an integral part of the Moors landscape rising from the highest ridges of moorland towards the sky like whales breaching the surface of an ocean. These mounds were not just burial sites but also marked out the territories of the Bronze Age tribes across the ridges of the moorland watersheds. Remarkably, many of the parish and estate boundaries of today are based upon these ancient Bronze Age tribal boundaries. Most of the burial mounds have been dug out and robbed of their treasures and so have the appearance of small bomb craters. The ashes of a tribal chieftain would have been buried in an urn or, very rarely, with more elaborate objects such as bronze daggers or an oak canoe. A retaining circular wall of standing stones would have been erected around this burial site and then covered with a mound of earth and stones; Simon Howe is still very impressive with several standing stones. According to local folklore these Howes are home to hobgoblins, the mischievous 'little people' that were often blamed for bad luck. The Lyke Wake Walk passes from west to east over Simon Howe, a gruelling 42-mile walk from Osmotherley to Ravenscar that tests the stamina of even the fittest walkers who endeavour to complete the walk within 24-hours. Many sections of the route are severely eroded as it crosses the central moorland with its fragile heather and peat covering.

Almost 35% of the North York Moors are covered by heather moorland, the largest expanse in England and Wales, almost all of which has been designated as a Site of Special Scientific Interest and a Special Protection Area under the EU Birds Directive as well as a Special Area of Conservation under the EU Habitats Directive. There are three main species of wild heather; the most common is Ling, which flowers in late summer, whilst Bell and Cross-leaved heather both flower a few weeks earlier. This heather landscape is entirely man-made and is managed through the rotational burning of large areas of moorland to encourage nutritious new growth for the grouse and sheep to feed on. However, as this moorland landscape is of international importance for its habitats and biodiversity, almost all of the heather moorland is now managed with conservation in mind. Natural England helps fund beneficial moorland management and conservation projects through their Environmental Stewardship Scheme, which aims to protect and enhance the landscape and its wildlife, as well as promote public access to the countryside, through initiatives including grazing management, bracken control, restricted heather burning and improved public access.

For eleven months of the year, especially during winter, the old name for this central moorland area seems very poignant – Blackamore. *"People talk about the 'purple' heather – as if that were the end of it all. The heather on the Goathland moors (using Goathland in the wider sense) passes through a hundred changes of colour between early summer and late autumn; from dull brown to green and then to the most exquisite tints of mauve, heliotrope, pinks, reds and russets; while the great belts of bracken change from green to gold and from gold to amber and bronze and russet. There seems to be no end to the delicate masses of colour that deck these moors in the fall of the year."* **(A. J. Brown 'Broad Acres' 1948)**. If you are fortunate enough to be blessed with a warm sunny day in early September then a walk across the moors will be an unforgettable experience with the delicate fragrance from millions of tiny flowers drifting with the breeze, a fine dust of pollen rising from the heather and the low hum of thousands of bees busily collecting pollen and nectar to make heather honey, renowned for its rich and distinctive flavour. Our path across this moor from Wardle Green, a rare place name that means 'valley of the Celts', once formed part of a medieval pannier-route between Malton and Whitby known as the Post Road. To the west of Simon Howe, across from the valley of Wheeldale Beck, is the expansive Wheeldale Moor. Here is an incredibly well-preserved section of Roman Road, the finest in the country, known as Wade's Causeway that runs for over a mile across the moor. Local legend would have us believe that this road was built by a giant called Wade as a path for his equally large wife to make her journey to market easier! *"It is loveliest here just before darkness comes, when shapes are softened in the evening light, and the moor seems to draw the road back to itself in sleep; but local people advise you not to stay too long on the moor at this time, for there are ghosts of more than Romans on it. Hob comes out to haunt the becks and bogs in a wraith of mist, and utters a peculiar cry which it is not lucky for men to hear."* **(E. Pontefract and M. Hartley 'Yorkshire Tour' 1939)**.

GOATHLAND was probably first settled by an Anglo-Scandinavian farmer called Goda over 1,000 years ago, although some historians claim the name of the village is derived from 'God's Land' as a hermitage dedicated to St Mary was established here in the 12th Century by King Henry I in what was the northern territory of the Forest of Pickering; what is certain is that the name has nothing to do with goats! There is no trace of the old hermitage, however, inside Goathland's church, which dates from 1896 and is also dedicated to St Mary, is an ancient stone altar inscribed with crosses that is thought to have come from this old religious site. Situated over 500 feet above sea level along a narrow strip of greenery between rolling moorland to the south and the ravines of West Beck and Eller Beck to the north, Goathland remained a dispersed farming hamlet until the arrival of the railway in 1836. *"...one of the few settlements which have not dived for cover in some sheltered valley. Instead it has elected to sit up apparently unperturbed on the flat moorland, taking its fill of the sharp clean air."* **(J. Herriot 'My Yorkshire' 1979)**.

George Stephenson's Whitby to Pickering Railway brought new life to Goathland in the form of tourists who came to marvel at its moorland setting and many waterfalls hidden away in the surrounding valleys. Of particular note is Mallyan Spout, a slender 70-foot cascade of water that falls over moss and fern covered rocks in a beautiful setting. The mile or so of rambling green between the church and the railway station soon began to be in-filled with large Victorian villas and hotels, with the older farms and cottages dotted conspicuously between. Goathland Station dates from 1865 when George Hudson upgraded the railway line to avoid the notorious Beck Hole 'Incline' with the construction of his 'Deviation Route' along the Eller Beck valley, although this section of line is still one of the steepest in the country. The Station and associated buildings are a classic example of North Eastern Railway design with the characteristic stepped gable ends. Although the track between Grosmont and Rillington fell victim to Beeching's axe in 1965, the 18-mile stretch between Grosmont and Pickering was brought back to life as the North Yorkshire Moors Railway a few years later. The attention to detail at Goathland Station is superb offering a glimpse of the 'golden age of steam' with waiting rooms, signal box and nostalgic bric-a-brac carefully positioned along the platform, not to mention the thrilling sight of a steam train pulling into the station. Adjacent to the Station is an old corn mill from where several paved trods radiate out across the village green. These flagged paths were laid down in the 17th Century and allowed farmers and villagers to walk to the local mill without having to use the muddy roads.

Above all, the reason why people are drawn to Goathland in their droves is the fact that it doubles as 'Aidensfield' in the long-running TV police drama series 'Heartbeat'. During the summer months car parks fill up very early and the rambling village green soon becomes thronged with families wandering aimlessly in search of 'Heartbeat', pausing outside Aidensfield Stores to have their pictures taken. Places you have never visited before feel familiar with an uneasy feeling of déjà vu at almost every corner. Television fame aside, Goathland has been attracting tourists for well over 100 years who come here to soak up its unique atmosphere. The soul of the village remains intact and a sense of excitement still hangs in the air when the weather draws in across the wild moors that reach into the village. Like so many of the remote places in the North York Moors, superstition lingered here long after it had died out elsewhere. Around 200 years ago a witch known as Nanny Pierson brought fear to the hearts of the people of Goathland, indeed it would appear that there were two witches of the same name in the village who were most probably successive generations of the same family. It is said that she could change herself into a hare at will and would cast spells that brought ill health or misfortune on local people. A more likely explanation is that in the days before education and medical discoveries an outbreak of disease or just plain bad luck would be blamed not upon nature but on a little old spinster. Goathland is also famous for its sword dance performed by the Goathland Plough Stots, first introduced to this area by the Vikings over 1,000 years ago. This dance combines the traditional sword dance with the pagan ritual of the blessing of the spring seeds, which was traditionally carried out by the Plough Stots on Plough Monday in January; 'stot' is the old word for a young bullock, which would have pulled the ploughs many centuries ago, later the name was given to the group of men who pulled the plough around the village. *"It is a hard unending struggle to wring a living from these moors, where communications are still difficult and visitors rare save in the few summer months. The struggle has produced a race apart, with its own speech and customs, its folklore and superstitions, and its odd survivals from a previous age, like the annual Plough Stots dance at Goathland, which celebrates the day on which the plough was put into the ground after the Deluge."* **(Harry Scott 'The English Counties' 1949)**.

DARNHOLME is an exquisite spot tucked away in the beautiful wooded valley of Eller Beck. A picture-postcard scene greets the eye as you drop down into this small hamlet, most of which lies out of sight on top of the small hill just to the west. Mellow stone cottages stand next to a watersplash, complete with stepping stones that ford Eller Beck, whilst all around is soft turf ideal for summer picnics. Eller Beck rises several miles to the south-east on Allerston High Moor and only becomes a valley of any note beyond Goathland when it is transformed from a gentle valley into a deep ravine. Eller Beck flows down to join forces with neighbouring West Beck just beyond Beck Hole to form the Murk Esk, one of Esk Dale's largest tributaries. Along this short stretch of fast-flowing river lie probably the greatest concentration of waterfalls within the North York Moors. Beneath the railway bridge with its skew arch, Eller Beck flows through a narrow chasm creating a treacherous force of water, especially after heavy rain; a sad memorial beside the river marks the spot where 16 year old Sydney Porritt drowned in 1908. Thomason Foss can be found just downstream from the incredible viaduct that towers above the river, an impressive waterfall with water plunging into a pool with overhanging rocks and trees; this waterfall is only accessible by way of a footpath from Beck Hole. Hudson's Deviation Route keeps us company for most of the way as it winds its way precariously above the narrow valley crossing and re-crossing the playful Eller Beck. This was a major feat of engineering that took four years to complete the 5-mile 'Deviation'; the original railway from Whitby to Pickering had only taken three years to build in its entirety. This new section of line required a major cutting, several bridges, the demolition and rebuilding of two farms and the re-routing of roads.

Darnholme

BECK HOLE, as the name implies, lies in a deep hollow near the confluence of Eller Beck and West Beck. The steep walk down along the road from the railway bridge gives a bird's eye view of the village green surrounded by a handful of attractive cottages, stone bridge and a traditional pub. In the early 17th Century Beck Hole comprised little more than a humble dwelling beside the ford across Eller Beck, however during the 1830s the Whitby to Pickering Railway was built passing through the Murk Esk valley with a station at Beck Hole. The arrival of the railway was the catalyst for change. The sleepy hamlet soon became a hive of industrial activity with ironstone and whinstone mines opening nearby as well as a number of blast furnaces. The population burgeoned to five times its present size with two inns to help quench the thirst of the miners: the Lord Nelson, which closed in 1940, and the Birch Hall Inn. This boom was short-lived, lasting less than a decade - only spoil heaps and one or two miners' cottages remain, however the Birch Hall Inn is still going strong. This inn became a full-time pub and village shop during the 1860s, a tradition still continued to this day. The present proprietors have been at the pub since 1981 when they bought it from Edith Schofield who had decided to retire after 53 years! Mrs Schofield sold it on the condition that the new owners would not change the layout of the pub; there was nothing further from their minds as they had bought it because of its layout. Another unique feature about this pub is its pub sign, which is a rather romantic painting of Eller Beck by Algernon Newton, a member of the Royal Academy who gave it to Mrs Schofield as a memento of many happy hours spent there. She then gave it to the whole village by fixing to the outside of the pub and naming it in the deeds.

The ancient game of quoits is played on the green; you may have noticed the rather large square coverings that protect the clay pitches. This game is still played in many villages throughout Esk Dale where teams from a thriving Quoits League compete over the summer months. It is a game of skill and strength that is said to have originated from when local farmers threw old horseshoes to pass the time whilst waiting for their horses to be shod. *"When the Beck Hole giants won the championship of the league recently against all comers there was a mighty celebration when they arrived home in their coach. To join them in the little friendly inn after a match, and watch them drink ale and play darts just as well as they play quoits, is a memorable experience. Usually they finish with a sing-song and nearly lift the roof off. Mrs Schofield, the popular landlady, knows how to deal with them all. Long may they flourish, these mighty blacksmiths and farmers of Beck Hole, who play quoits and darts like champions."* **(A. J. Brown 'Fair North Riding' 1952).**

Birch Hall Inn

Most people arrive in Beck Hole on foot after following the waymarked Rail Trail from Grosmont to Goathland and then catch the steam train home, a pleasant journey indeed. The highlight of this walk is the famous Beck Hole 'Incline'. This mile long hill once formed part of Stephenson's original railway, climbing up a staggering 1 in 10 gradient into Goathland. Carriages were hauled up this incline by a complex system of ropes, pulleys and water tanks. Accidents, as you might imagine, were commonplace, however the Incline became something of a tourist attraction with even Charles Dickens writing about his enjoyable trip along the railway. All this came to an end following a terrible accident in 1864 when the rope snapped and carriages went careering downhill killing two and injuring thirteen passengers - Hudson's 'Deviation Route' opened the following year. The Incline was reopened between 1908 and 1914 as an Autocar service during the summer months for Edwardian tourists who came to soak up the natural beauty of the area. Our route follows a section of Stephenson's original railway along the old cinder track-bed, passing through ancient woodland with the delightful Murk Esk as company.

EGTON BRIDGE lies at the heart of Esk Dale, a valley of pure delight and variety from its source high amongst the wild moors of Westerdale to the wonderful old fishing town of Whitby where it disappears into the North Sea. Esk Dale also flows west to east, unlike any other major valley in the North York Moors. For me, the real charm of Esk Dale are the numerous tributaries that feed the valley from its southern side, each with their own distinct character. *"There was the long valley, running east and west, which had seemed so narrow when beheld from the grudging heights above, and which was now seen to be from a mile to a mile and a half broad, and with dale after dale, not wide but long and deep, opening into it from its southern side. High on either side of each of these dales towered the moorland banks, and along each dale I could trace the course of a minor stream, with its fringe of trees, running its descending race towards the main stream in the longer or medial valley. There was verdure everywhere, with plentiful signs of careful tillage, and the luxuriant growth springing from a grateful soil. It might be that, having had the wild wilderness of the brown moor around me for so long, the eye was doubly grateful for the fresh greens of the beck-side pastures and the widely-spread green crops. But with colour, contrast, and contour, soaring hill and deepening dale, abrupt nab-end and craggy wood, all* *claiming notice at once, rather than in their proper turn, the scene spread before me was something more than simply beautiful."* **(Rev. J. C. Atkinson 'Forty Years in a Moorland Parish' 1891).** Egton Bridge is the jewel in the crown of this wonderful valley and is considered by many, including me, to be one of the prettiest villages in Yorkshire. The sheer pleasure of walking along the pavement of well-worn stone flags, passing elegant houses with manicured gardens for a well-earned pint on a mellow summer's evening after walking from Levisham is one of life's rich and happy experiences.

Egton Bridge began life, as the name would suggest, adjacent to the river crossing over the Esk whilst Egton (on the hill) is the original and much older settlement. The steep road that connects the two villages is said to be haunted by a Barguest, a spectral black hound with large red eyes and a blood-curdling howl, the sight of which is said to be an omen of death. Stories of such creatures abound throughout Yorkshire and probably entered our folklore from the Viking settlers. The River Esk flows through the heart of Egton Bridge, one of the few remaining salmon rivers left in this country, with a double set of stepping stones leading from the Horseshoe Hotel to an old corn mill via a small wooded island mid-stream; it is a thrilling sight indeed to watch salmon leaping this weir in season. *"We should stay a while at Egton Bridge, which is a lovely spot. Pretty cottages and wooded banks, so common in the dales, abound here, but the beauty of the place is enhanced a thousand fold by the noble river which, though broad, is here very charming."* **(A. P. Wilson 'Yorkshire Moors and Dales' 1910).** The original stone bridge of 1758 was washed away by floods in 1930, after which a temporary iron bridge was hastily constructed that lasted until the new award-winning stone bridge was erected in 1993, built to look like the old 18th Century bridge. The Esk Valley Railway arrived at Egton Bridge in 1865, connecting the Whitby to Pickering line at Grosmont to Middlesbrough via Battersby Junction. The Esk Valley Railway was saved from Beeching's infamous axe due to the concerted efforts of people from Whitby and Esk Dale who feared the loss of an essential lifeline to the outside world. Many of the houses in the village date from this time as wealthy people moved to the area. The Postgate Inn along with the adjacent row of cottages were built at the same time as the station and clearly stand out due to their Victorian 'railway' architecture. An interesting relic of the days of steam engines can be found in the car park adjacent to the village school. These Coal Cells were managed by the Station Master who would store coal according to its quality in different bunkers to be sold to local farmers and businesses, the proceeds from which he would keep. So lucrative was this that they often refused promotion due to the cut in income! In the heart of the village stands Egton Manor, an elegant Victorian and Edwardian house set in beautiful gardens; the house and gardens are in private ownership (no access). A permissive path, known as the Old Toll Road, leads from Egton Bridge through the grounds of Egton Manor to Grosmont; look out for the old sign displaying the toll charges in shillings and pence!

The people of the North York Moors were slow to give up the Old Faith following the Dissolution of the Monasteries. Nonconformist worship gained a strong foothold in the area with many people turning away from the 'new' Established Church in favour of Nonconformist teachings. However, the Reformation appears to have missed this secluded part of Esk Dale making Egton Bridge one of the most famous Catholic parishes in England. The continuation of the Catholic faith can be attributed to Father Nicholas Postgate, the 'Martyr of the Moors'. Hailing from Egton Bridge, Father Postgate travelled to France to train as a Catholic priest (Catholicism was banned in England at that time) and returned to Yorkshire to travel the moorland tracks, often disguised as a poor man, to celebrate mass in isolated farms. A house situated almost at the top of the steep hill up to Egton is known as the Mass House, as this was where Father Postgate held Mass in a secret room. The danger for practising Catholics worsened following the Popish Plot against King Charles II in 1678 when rewards were offered for information about their whereabouts. This temptation proved too much for John Reeves, a local man who informed the authorities about Father Postgate who was planning to baptise a child into the Catholic faith. Father

Postgate was arrested and tried for treason in 1679, when he was 82 - he was taken to York and hung, drawn and quartered. Overcome with guilt, Reeves was later found drowned in a nearby river at a spot known as Devil's Hole where, it is said, no fish have been caught since. The imposing Catholic Church dedicated to St Hedda was built in 1866 and has a wonderfully ornate altar and a striking blue ceiling. There are also numerous three-dimensional wall pictures inside and out depicting the Stations of the Cross and life of Jesus.

In the shadow of the church stands the much smaller original church that was built in 1795 and now serves as the village school and home of the famous Egton Bridge Annual Gooseberry Show. The Egton Bridge Old Gooseberry Society was established in 1800 and hold their famous annual Gooseberry Show every August when 'goosegogs' the size of golf balls are proudly exhibited, subject to very strict Society rules. This unique event is one of the oldest agricultural shows in England.

EGTON BRIDGE
to
ROSEDALE ABBEY

✦

"The central high moors above Rosedale are wild and desolate. There is no shelter, no escape from storm or shine. Grouse hide amongst the thick heather, only taking flight seconds before standing on them, their loud 'cackle' coupled with flapping wings gives fright and makes your heart pound. An old trod, paved for most of the way with stone blocks worn by centuries of use, leads unerringly across the open moorland gently winding left then right. Clouds on the horizon are soon over us, reducing visibility to a matter of yards. Out of the swirling mist a slender silhouette gradually appears. A weathered moorland cross, crudely fashioned from two or three smaller blocks of sandstone, brings a moment of relief and reassurance, as if the Guardian of the Moors is looking over us. Two or three hundred years ago trains of packhorses carrying fish from Staithes or coal from moorland pits came this way across a moorland scene similar to that of today. It is a relief, just as it was all those years ago, to drop down out of the mist into the relative safety of Rosedale for food and shelter."

Mark Reid
March 2000

WALK INFORMATION

Points of interest: Paved pannierways, a 'romantic' bridge, the pretty village hidden 'amongst the twigs', a dramatic bird's eye view of Great Fryup Dale, walking the Motorways of the Middle Ages, ironstone relics, railways in the sky and the ruins of Rosedale's Priory.

Distance:

Egton Bridge to Lealholm	4.5 miles
Lealholm to Rosedale Abbey	10.5 miles
Total	15 miles

Time: Allow 7 hours

Terrain: A variety of terrain is encountered along this walk with field, woodland and riverside paths and tracks through Esk Dale, stone-paved 'trods' through Arncliffe Wood and across Glaisdale Moor (George Gap Causeway) as well as clear tracks across Glaisdale Rigg, around the head of Great Fryup Dale and along the length of Rosedale. The undulating path through Esk Dale includes a number of 'short but sharp' ascents and descents. The high moorland between Esk Dale and Rosedale can be boggy underfoot with several small stream crossings, and is exposed to the elements. The clear tracks and paths means that route finding across Glaisdale Moor is relatively straight-forward; however, navigation may be difficult in mist. The ascent from Lealholm to the head of Great Fryup Dale is long and gradual, whilst the descent into Rosedale is quite steep in places.

The paths and tracks across Glaisdale Moor are boggy and exposed to the elements, whilst route finding across this moorland may be difficult in poor weather.

Take care walking along the minor roads through Esk Dale and across Glaisdale Rigg. There are a number of short but steep sections along this walk.

| Ascents: | Loose Howe, Glaisdale Moor: 410 metres |

Viewpoints: Glaisdale Rigg looking across Glaisdale.
Cut Road affords incredible views down Great Fryup Dale.
Views across Glaisdale Moor and Rosedale Moor from George Gap Causeway.
Descent along George Gap Causeway offers thrilling views of Rosedale.

FACILITIES

Egton Bridge	Inn / B&B / Bus / Train / Phone / Toilets
Glaisdale	Inn / B&B / Shop / P.O. / Bus / Train / Phone / Toilets
Lealholm	Inn / B&B / Shop / P.O. / Café / Bus / Train / Phone / Toilets
Rosedale Abbey	Inn / B&B / Shop / Café / Bus / Phone / Toilets / Camp

ROUTE DESCRIPTION

(Map Ten)

Leave Egton Bridge up along the road towards 'Goathland' from the road junction near the Horseshoe Hotel. After approx. 100 yards take the FP to the right (SP 'Delves') along a leafy track which quickly leads to a stile over a fence, after which head left up the hillside alongside the tumbledown wall/hedge on your left. You soon cross over a small stream, after which continue climbing quite steeply up the hillside alongside this wooded stream on your left to reach a stile in the top corner of the field (at the top of the hill). After the stile, head straight on across the field bearing very slightly to the right to reach a stile that leads onto a grassy track (NZ 801 047). Turn right along this tree-shaded track and follow it straight on for 150 yards to reach a fork in the track, where you carry straight on along the right-hand enclosed tree-shaded track for a further 100 yards then, where the track opens out slightly, follow it curving gently round to the left to soon reach a gate in a wall across your path. After this gate, carry straight on along the grassy track across the field (partly enclosed by trees) to reach a stone barn on your left. Walk past the barn then immediately turn right down the hillside keeping the overgrown hedge on your right to reach a gate at the bottom of the field beside Hall Grange Farm (NZ 797 043). Head through the gate to quickly join the farm track where you turn right through the farmyard (passing the farmhouse on your right) and continue along the track for approx. 250 yards then take the FP on the left over a stile (SP) into woods. Follow the path down the hillside, over a wide bridge across a small stream then straight on across the field, keeping the hedge on your right, and down to reach a gateway tucked away in the corner of the field (hidden amongst trees). After the gateway, head to the left across the field and drop down to cross Butter Beck over a FB, after which head straight up the hillside climbing quite steeply up alongside the edge of the field (and small stream) on your right to reach a wall across your path at the top of the field. Cross the stile over this wall (SP) and head up to quickly reach a gate in another wall that leads onto a track, with the farmhouse of The Delves just to your right. Cross over the track and follow the FP directly opposite through a small gate/stile (SP 'Delves Farm'), after which bear to the right up through the trees to soon reach an old stone wall across your path (at the top of the thick woods). Cross over this wall, then continue straight on up across the sparsely wooded hillside for a short distance then bear slightly right up through the trees to reach a gate in the top right corner of the field that leads onto the road at Delves (NZ 791 045).

Turn right along the road heading steeply down, winding past the houses at Delves then, as the road begins to level out, take the track to the left ('No Vehicles') that leads into Arncliffe Wood. Follow the clear, wide path straight on meandering through the woods. After 0.5 miles, the River Esk comes into view down to your right and the path becomes paved underfoot - carry straight on along the stone-paved path gradually dropping down through the woods for a further 0.25 miles down to join the banks of the Esk on your right where you follow the riverside path straight on for another 0.25 miles to join a clear track across your path beside a ford/FB across Glaisdale Beck just to your right, beyond which are the railway bridge and then Beggar's Bridge across the River Esk (NZ 784 055).

Turn left along the track *(do not cross the ford/FB)* for a short distance to reach a fork in the track (beside the house on your right) where you bear right down over a FB across Glaisdale Beck then up along the rough track to reach the road beside the Arncliffe Arms at Carr End. At the road take the lane directly opposite ('Local Traffic Only') and follow this straight on for 0.25 miles before climbing steeply up into Glaisdale. Just before the top of the hill where the road bends round to the left, take the track to the right immediately after Wrens Nest House through a gate (SP) that leads into Millers Wood (NZ 777 055). Follow the track down through the woods to reach the old mill beside the River Esk. As you reach the old mill (house), carry straight on along the path that passes to the left-hand side of the house then, just after the house and garden, turn right *(do not climb steps into woods)* to join a riverside path (just behind the old mill). Follow this path through woodland alongside the River Esk on your right to reach a stile at the end of the woods, after which head to the left across the field (still with the river just to your right) then, where the river turns away under the railway bridge, head straight on to cross a stile by a gate. After this stile head straight on bearing slightly to the right to join the railway embankment on your right which you follow straight on up to reach a stile in the corner of the field (beside the railway line). Cross the railway line *(take care)* and over the stile on the opposite side of the tracks, then turn left across the field and up to reach a stile just to the right of the old stone railway bridge *(Waddell Railway)* that leads onto the road opposite Rake Farm (NZ 778 066).

Turn left along the road over the old bridge *(Waddell Railway)* and then the railway bridge *(Esk Valley line)* then, as the road bends to the left, turn right along a rough track (SP 'Lealholm') that leads quite steeply down to a FB/ford over the River Esk. After the FB, head left along the grassy track and follow this straight on across the field then, as you re-join the River Esk after 150 yards, follow the track bending round to the right then take the FP to the left (SP) immediately before the hump-backed bridge over the railway. Follow the path through woodland at first then down to join the riverbank, which you follow all the way (river on your left) to reach a gate just to the left of the large barns at Underpark Farm (NZ 772 070). Head through the gate and follow the track round to the right through the farmyard (skirting to the left of the barns) to reach a junction of tracks (farmhouse just to your right) where you turn left along the track (SP) and follow it for 0.75 miles all the way into Lealholm.

(Map Eleven)

As you emerge in the centre of Lealholm, turn left along the road (SP 'Glaisdale 2'), over the road-bridge across the River Esk passing the pub on your right and out of the village. Continue straight on along this road for 1.25 miles rising steadily up (passing Mill Lane Farm on your left after 0.5 miles) until you come to a crossroads. At this crossroads, continue straight on along the road ahead towards 'Rosedale' (sign 'Unsuitable for Coaches, Caravans and HGV's') then, after approx. 400 yards, take the second FP to the left (SP 'Glaisdale Rigg') just below numerous small mounds (old workings) on the moorland just ahead (NZ 749 060). Follow the narrow path bearing gradually away from the road across the open moorland passing to the left of (just below) these small mounds, keeping to roughly the same contour line across the hillside. Beyond these mounds, continue straight on along the narrow path across the moorland (still keeping to the same contour line) for a further 0.5 miles (path becomes sunken for a while then gradually becomes less distinct and boggy) to reach a small stone-slab FB over Busco Beck marked by two stone posts. After the FB, head straight on up across the moor along a path marked by two standing stones for 0.3 miles up to the top of the ridge where you come to a rough track across your path. Cross over this track and head straight on across the moorland to quickly reach the clearer track along Glaisdale Rigg, marked by a SP (NZ 749 046). Turn right here and follow the track up for 0.75 miles to reach the road. At the road head straight on along the unfenced moorland road across the top of the broad moorland ridge of Glaisdale Rigg. After 0.5 miles follow the unfenced road down into a slight 'dip' *(junction of paths and tracks at the bottom of this slight dip – Hart Leap Stones just to your left)* where you carry straight on along the unfenced road gradually rising up across the top of Glaisdale Rigg for a further 0.5 miles to reach a track off to the right (SP) guarded by a conspicuous wooden gate (NZ 729 028). After the gate, bear slightly left and follow the clear path that leads across the heather moorland gradually bearing away from the unfenced road *(this path runs parallel with the shooters' track just to your right)*. Follow this clear, wide path (Cut Road) straight on across Glaisdale Moor for 0.5 miles until the upper reaches of Great Fryup Dale come into view down to your right. Continue straight on along the clear path across the moorland, with Great Fryup Dale falling away down to your right, for a further 0.5 miles then follow the path gradually curving round to the right around the head of the valley until you reach a large pile of stones (cairn) at the head of the valley (NZ 715 017).

(Map Twelve)

Continue along the path past this cairn for approx. 100 yards then take the BW to the left (SP) marked by a small cairn. A clear path, paved for long stretches (George Gap Causeway), meanders across the moor for 0.75 miles to reach the eroded route of the Lyke Wake Walk across your path (white-topped boundary stones), where you carry straight on along the stone-paved path for a further 0.3 miles before passing between old workings on the left and Loose Howe up to the right to reach an unfenced moorland road (NZ 703 006). Cross over the road along the path directly opposite (SP 'Rosedale'), and follow this straight on across the moorland gently dropping down towards

Rosedale (passing two boundary stones along the way) for 0.3 miles to reach a stream set in a small ravine. Cross the stream then follow the path round to the left then straight down the steep hillside alongside this ravine on your left (ravine becomes much more pronounced) to reach the old Rosedale Ironstone railway track-bed across your path (SE 698 998). Cross over the old railway embankment and follow the rough grassy track opposite that bears down the hillside to the right passing a small plantation on your left to reach a gate in a fence across your path (plantation on your left). Head through the gate and continue down the track for a short distance then, at the next gate in the stone wall, turn down to the left *(do not head through the gate)* along a sparsely wooded sunken path (stream to your left) that leads down to join the road at Dale Head Farm (SE 695 993). Turn left down along the road for a short distance then head right (SP) through a small gate (just before the road-bridge across the stream) and follow the path across the field, through another gate then head straight on across the middle of the field bearing slightly to the right (passing to the right of the telegraph pole) to reach a FB across the River Seven almost in the far right-hand corner of the field. Cross the FB and head straight up the hillside to a gate in the top right-hand corner of the field that leads onto a track beside Hollin Bush Farm (SE 691 991).

Turn left along the track then follow it bending round to the left after a short distance to soon reach the cluster of buildings at Moorlands Farm where you follow the road down to the left. After approx. 150 yards take the grassy track to the right through a gate (SP) and follow this clear track (Daleside Road) straight on heading down through Rosedale, gradually becoming clearer, for just under 1 mile to reach a farmhouse on your right (The Alders) where you continue straight on along the track to quickly join a clear stony track just beyond the farm buildings (that leads from the farmhouse - SE 697 976). Follow this clear track straight on (to the left) for a further mile to reach the cluster of houses at Thorgill where the track becomes a metalled lane. Continue along this road passing through Thorgill, down over a wide bridge across a stream and follow the road up for a short distance then bending sharply round to the left passing Crag View (house) on the corner. After Crag View, continue along the road gradually curving round to the right for almost 0.5 miles then take the FP to the left through a kissing gate in a stone wall (just before the road begins to gradually rise up), marked by a SP (SE 715 964). After the kissing-gate, follow the path straight on down across middle of the field and through a gate that leads into woodland and down to reach a FB across the River Seven. After the FB turn left then immediately right along a clear path to quickly reach a bridlegate at the end of the woods. After the bridlegate, head straight on across the field alongside the fence/wooded bank on your left for approx. 50 yards then follow the path slanting to the left up this bank then, where the fence turns away to the left, carry straight on across the hillside to soon join another fence/woodland on your right. Follow this fence straight on for 0.25 miles across fields to reach a gate that leads into a caravan site. Follow the road straight on through the caravan site then take the FP to the left after the play area (but before the stone house) to quickly reach a stone wall stile that leads onto the road in the centre of Rosedale Abbey.

Rosedale Ironstone Kilns

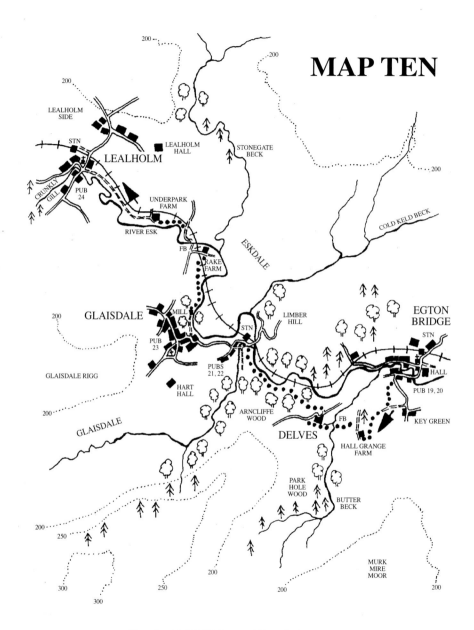

MAP TEN

MAP ELEVEN

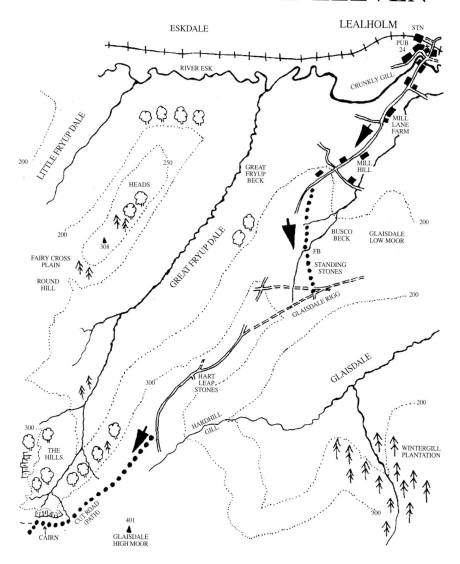

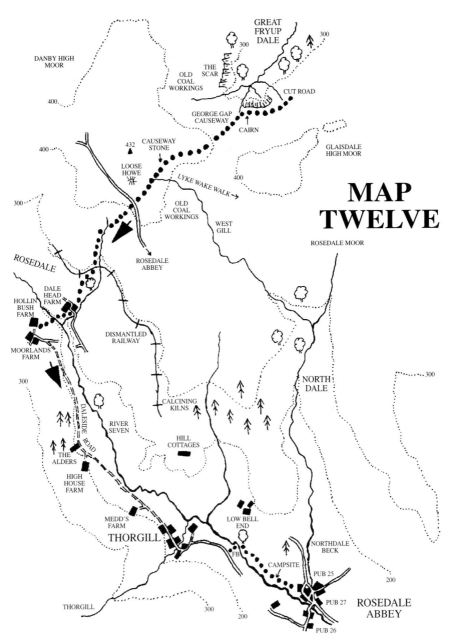

GREAT FRYUP DALE

300

DANBY HIGH MOOR

THE SCAR

OLD COAL WORKINGS

300

CUT ROAD

400

GEORGE GAP CAUSEWAY

CAIRN

432

CAUSEWAY STONE

400

GLAISDALE HIGH MOOR

LOOSE HOWE

LYKE WAKE WALK →

400

300

OLD COAL WORKINGS

WEST GILL

MAP TWELVE

ROSEDALE MOOR

ROSEDALE

ROSEDALE ABBEY

DALE HEAD FARM

HOLLIN BUSH FARM

DISMANTLED RAILWAY

MOORLANDS FARM

300

NORTH DALE

300

CALCINING KILNS

RIVER SEVEN

DALESIDE ROAD

THE ALDERS

HILL COTTAGES

HIGH HOUSE FARM

MEDD'S FARM

LOW BELL END

THORGILL

FB

NORTHDALE BECK

CAMPSITE

PUB 25

200

THORGILL

300

200

PUB 27

ROSEDALE ABBEY

PUB 26

ARNCLIFFE WOOD, or Arnecliff on maps, is an ancient piece of woodland along the steep banks of the River Esk, an absolute delight to walk through especially in spring or autumn when the colours are at their very best. An old pannierway leads through these woods, paved for much of the way, from Delves to Beggar's Bridge; 'delves' is an old word for the pits created by primitive ironstone mining. The path meanders leisurely through the woods and many of the paving stones have been worn down by centuries of use since at least the 17th Century. These were once important trading routes along which lines of packhorses laden with everything from fish to coal, ironstone, salt, jet, charcoal and lime would walk in single file, thus avoiding the unmade and often impassable roads. Look out for the Kid Stone; 'kid' was the term for bundles of firewood which were placed on this large stone before being loaded onto a waiting packhorse. Nearby is the Wishing Stone, a large bolder with a deep cleft that has split it in two through which a tree once grew; it is said that if you walk around it three times then your wish will come true!

BEGGAR'S BRIDGE is a graceful 17th Century packhorse bridge that spans the River Esk, a bridge that gave rise to a romantic story. Thomas Ferris (sometimes Ferries) was the son of a poor farmer, who was courting a local beauty Agnes Richardson, the daughter of a wealthy landowner who, needless to say, did not approve of such shenanigans. Thomas regularly made the short journey across the River Esk from Glaisdale to see his sweetheart; however, in order to win her hand he decided to go to sea to make his fortune. The night before he was due to leave Thomas set out in torrential rain to see Agnes but was prevented from crossing the swollen River Esk due to the raging torrents of water. So Thomas went to sea, fought against the Armada and made his fortune - although some say through piracy. He returned to Glaisdale a rich man and married Agnes, later settling at Hull where he became a wealthy shipping merchant as well as the Lord Mayor. He built this graceful bridge in 1619 so that no other lovers would be separated by the river, although it was perhaps more of a memorial to Agnes who died in 1618; the initial 'T F' and the date '1619' can be seen on the parapet. *"If you ask anyone in Whitby* *to mention some of the sights of the neighbourhood, he will probably head his list with the Beggar's Bridge, but why this is so I cannot imagine. The woods are very beautiful, but this is a country full of the loveliest dales, and the presence of this single-arched bridge does not seem sufficient to have attracted so much popularity. I can only attribute it to the love interest associated with the beggar."* **(G. Home 'Yorkshire' 1908).** Just along the road from Beggar's Bridge towards Glaisdale Station is a row of Coal Cells similar to those at Egton Bridge.

GLAISDALE, from the Celtic word 'glas' meaning 'fresh or blue', is a sprawling village built on steep hills at the point where the valleys of Glaisdale and Esk Dale meet. The steep walk up into the main village will reveal an amazing assortment of houses including stone miners' cottages, old farms, Victorian terraces and large brick houses; Glaisdale has the feel of an industrial town rather than a rural village. The reason for this was the arrival in 1865 of the railway and the subsequent development of ironstone mining in the hills behind the village, thus changing its character forever. The mines may have closed over 100 years ago but the village remains a busy place with three pubs *(sadly, two now closed)*, shops, Post Office, Methodist Church and school. Most amazingly of all, Glaisdale is still the home of the Glaisdale and Lealholm Association for the Prosecution of Felons, or 'The Felons' for short. This society dates from medieval times when local people sought to protect themselves and their livestock against crime long before policemen pounded the beat, and it is said to be the last of its kind in the country. No one can remember the last time it actually brought a felon to task and it would appear that its sole purpose is an annual dinner! The Church of St Thomas the Apostle dates from the 16th Century although there has almost certainly been a Chapel-of-Ease here since the 14th Century. The church was rebuilt in 1793 and restored again in 1868; look out for the original datestone of 1585 set into the steps near to the main entrance. Thomas Ferris, builder of the romantic Beggar's Bridge, remembered this small church in his will and provided bequests for the upkeep of the chapel; his portrait can be seen in the church.

Ironstone has been mined on the North York Moors since the Iron Age, although small-scale organised production began in the 13th Century by the large monastic houses; indeed in 1223 monks from Guisborough Priory were smelting iron at Glaisdale, all of which came to an end with the Dissolution of the Monasteries. The onset of the Industrial Revolution in the early 19th Century brought with it a renewed interest in the iron industry, which hit the North York Moors with a 'bang' during the 1830s when a rich seam of ironstone was discovered at Grosmont during construction work for the Whitby to Pickering Railway. In 1865 this railway was extended from Grosmont to Teesside via Esk Dale and in the following year the Glaisdale Drift Mines were opened by Firth and Hodgson & Co to the south of the village. Glaisdale was now an industrial town with miners' cottages, grime, noise and a population level twice that of today. Production increased during the early 1870s and a shaft over 250-ft deep was excavated which enabled the ironstone to be taken quickly from the mines straight to the three blast furnaces in the valley bottom. However, the seams were poor and the ironworks closed in 1876 due to a slump in the market. Only scars, spoil heaps and a number of miners' cottages remain as a reminder of this small but important contribution to the Industrial Revolution.

Just to the south of the village is Hart Hall Farm, which has entered local folklore due to its helpful hobgoblin. This secretive Hob worked on the farm in the dead of night helping the farmer with tasks, which were often too much for several strong men. One night a local lad decided to have a sneaky look at the Hob who was busy working in one of the barns dressed only in a few ragged clothes. The next day he told the farmer and his friends what he had seen and so they decided to make some new clothes for this little man as a goodwill gesture. The clothes were duly left outside the barn one evening; however, the Hob saw the clothes and realised that they had been spying on him and so left the farm forever. There is a moral in that tale somewhere! *But we left our old lady in the midst of her "Hob" reminiscences, which, as I have said, and emphasised in the last chapter, she told with a sort of personal recollection of them, rather than as what had been told her by others, or handed down from one teller of the old, old story to another."* **(Rev. J. C. Atkinson 'Forty Years in a Moorland Parish' 1891)**. Our route leaves Glaisdale through Millers' Wood passing an old corn mill, complete with waterwheel, which has an idyllic setting amongst trees beside the River Esk.

THE PADDY WADDELL RAILWAY, officially known as the Cleveland Mineral Extension Railway, was an ambitious project to take a branch line from the Esk Valley Railway near Rake Farm over the moors to connect with railway lines near Lingdale over ten miles away to the north. In 1873 John Waddell, a famous Victorian railway engineer, began work on this line which was intended to provide a more direct route to the mines and furnaces at Glaisdale. The closure of the Glaisdale ironworks did not help, nor did the end of the railway 'boom years', however, this project continued on and off until 1896. Cuttings, embankments and foundations can be seen along most of its intended route, though tracks were never laid. An overgrown and waterlogged cutting as well as a railway bridge can clearly be seen near Rake Farm, which served as a pub during the 'construction' years. John Waddell was nicknamed Paddy after the many Irish navvies he employed.

LEALHOLM, pronounced locally 'Lealum', could easily be described as the perfect English country village. The River Esk flows leisurely through the village, spanned by an 18th Century stone bridge beside which stands the village pub. The curving river looks inviting for a swim, but beware - strong currents have undercut the riverbank beneath the surface and it has been the scene of fatal accidents in recent years. Quoits is played on the village green which, along with common land in the area, is administered by the ancient Danby Court Leet, a medieval manorial court with similar powers to the Court Leet of the Manor of Spaunton. Village life is thriving here with an amazingly well stocked shop, train station, Post Office, tea rooms, school, garage and churches of various denominations including Catholic, Anglican and Methodist. The Church of St James the Greater, noted for its very thin tower, was designed by Temple Moore and dates from 1902, whilst the Wesleyan (Methodist) Chapel of 1839 boasts stonework on its gable ends by local stonemason John Castillo, who was also known as the 'Poet of the Moors'. Pause to notice the stone tablet on the side of the Methodist Chapel that records the height of two notable floods in July 1840 and July 1930. A path leads down the side of this chapel to stepping-stones across the Esk, exciting to say the least after heavy rain. Unbelievably, local farmers used this short cut to get to their fields followed by a flock of sheep! Other buildings of note in the village include the old Loyal Order of Ancient Shepherds Friendly Society Hall, now the tea rooms, which operated as a type of insurance company for local people before the days of Social Security, opposite which stands an old mill complete with mill race flowing beneath it.

Look out for the three elegant water fountains throughout the village. These were 'given' to the village along with the first piped water supply in 1904 by Sir Francis Ley, a wealthy Nottingham lace maker who owned the Estate a century ago. Ley also built a number of attractive cottages and laid out Crunkly Gill to the west of the village with paths, plants and trees although the flood of 1930 destroyed much of his handiwork. This precipitous gorge was carved out by glacial meltwaters during the last Ice Age when a huge lake filled upper Esk Dale above Lealholm, downstream from which floodwaters cascaded carving many deep gorges and channels, which explains why the road does not follow the valley floor to the east of Lealholm but twists up and down the valley sides. Crunkly Gill still boasts many rare plants and fine trees and is often referred to as the 'largest rock garden in England', although it is a dangerous place to explore with no Rights of Way. Incidentally, Lealholm's unusual name originates from old Saxon words meaning 'amongst the twigs', which is still an apt description.

GLAISDALE RIGG is a high heather-clad finger of land that reaches out from the central moorland into Esk Dale. 'Rigg' is the local term for the gently sloping and rising ridges that divide the numerous valleys of the North York Moors, many of which are littered with Bronze and Iron Age remains. Ancient trading routes also cross these ridges as the high ground avoided the swampy and often dangerous valley floors; look out for the old guideposts alongside the road, which was once an important route to and from Whitby. It is always a pleasure to walk across this ridge with heather underfoot and wonderful views either side of you into deep valleys. *"Yet I would not advise the traveller to cling to the dales alone. He should venture on the high ground overlooking sea and valley, and he will be rewarded by delightful views of both. From many of the heights in the valley of the Esk magnificent views of the sea can be obtained; and everyone knows how delightful it is, when walking on the moor, to come suddenly upon some lovely green and cultivated valley spreading out at one's feet."* **(A. P. Wilson 'Yorkshire Moors and Dales' 1910).** High on Glaisdale Rigg are the famous Hart Leap Stones, two small stones hidden in heather just off the road near a junction of paths, tracks and bridleways. The stones are set 40-foot apart and, according to local legend, mark the spot where a large stag made its last leap in a vain attempt to escape the huntsmen and their hounds; one stone marks where the stag took off and the other where it landed. In truth, they are more likely to be prehistoric standing stones.

GREAT FRYUP DALE is one of the finest valleys in the North York Moors, the name of which always brings a smile to your face - it has nothing to do with the breakfast fare at local B&B's but is derived from 'Friga', an old Saxon personal name, and 'hop' meaning valley. *"Do not ask me why it is called Fryup, or why near Fryup Hall you will pass Fairy Cross Plain, because, disregarding all Scandinavian origins and myths, I can only tell you that when the early Yorkshire settlers came to these parts they became famous for their expert manipulation of the frying-pan, especially in the matter of ham and eggs, which was their staple diet."* **(A. J. Brown 'Fair North Riding' 1952).** An old track, known as Cut Road, skirts the head of Great Fryup Dale to join the Danby road high on the moors near Trough House, an area littered with primitive coal workings. During the 18th and early 19th centuries there were numerous small coalfields throughout the North York Moors which produced poor quality coal for the fledgling ironstone industry, limestone kilns and also for domestic use, however they soon closed in favour of the much larger Durham and Northumberland coalfields. The view from this track looking down the length of Great Fryup Dale is incredible with plunging waterfalls, precipitous crags and wooded ravines falling away from beneath your feet, a scene reminiscent of the Lake District. The large hill that divides Great Fryup Dale from Little Fryup Dale is called Heads, whilst the 'saddle' of land that offers a peek into this smaller sister valley is known as Fairy Cross Plain with its bright green fields and peculiar Round Hill where fairies are said to live! *"Among others, a man with whom I was brought into perpetual contact, from the relative positions we occupied in the parish – he was, and is, parish clerk – had told me that his childhood had been spent in the immediate vicinity of "the Plains", and that the fairy-rings just above the inn in question were the largest and the most regular and distinct he had ever seen anywhere. He and the other children of the hamlet used constantly to amuse themselves by running round and round in these rings; but they had always been religiously careful never to run quite nine times round any one of them."* **(Rev. J. C. Atkinson 'Forty Years in a Moorland Parish' 1891).**

GEORGE GAP CAUSEWAY was once the longest paved causeway in the North York Moors stretching from Lealholm to the Blakey Ridge Road, a busy trading route that linked the coastal ports of Staithes and Whitby with the market town of Kirkbymoorside and York. The majority of these causeways, or trods, date from the 17th Century as trade in commodities such as fish, salt and coal began to increase hand in hand with the prosperity of the country. These trods allowed quicker access to markets than the unmade roads - fresh fish could be taken to York within a day - and were still in use in the late 19th Century until better roads and railways made them obsolete. What a sight it must have been to see a train of up to forty packhorses moving in single file across the moors carrying coal from the moorland pits. George Gap Causeway, still paved for most of the way, leads from the head of Great Fryup Dale over Glaisdale Moor to Rosedale with far-reaching views of the rolling moors stretching hazily into the distance. Look out for the occasional stone guidepost inscribed with the words 'Rosdal' and 'Whitby' as well as boundary stones; the badly eroded route of the Lyke Wake Walk crosses our path by the white-capped Causeway Stone. As the path nears the metalled road note the numerous old coal pits on the left, whilst on the higher ground to your right is Loose Howe. This conspicuous Bronze Age burial mound was excavated in 1937 and found to contain an oak coffin in the shape of a canoe, bronze dagger, pottery, stone axe and human ashes dating back almost 4,000 years.

ROSEDALE lies at the heart of the moors, a deep valley of great beauty that appears to have been scooped out of the central moorland with wooded pastures that sweep up to rocky outcrops and the wild moors that surround the head of the dale. All around are the scars of the old ironstone mines and works; the wounds are slow to heal. These scars have become an accepted part of the landscape and add a fascinating dimension to the valley. The name of the valley is derived from 'Russi', an old Scandinavian farmer's name who settled in this valley many centuries ago. Rosedale runs for about eight miles from Rosedale Head to Hartoft End where the valley narrows and 'Rosedale' ends, although the River Seven continues for many more miles to flow into the River Rye in the Vale of Pickering. Most people associate ironstone mining with Rosedale, but the valley was also the home of another industry that remained a secret for almost four hundred years. In Elizabethan times skilled glass makers came to this secluded valley to produce glass illegally, for glass making was then only carried out by craftsmen who held special licences and so many glass makers went 'underground'. In 1968 the extensive remains of an Elizabethan glass furnace were found on Spaunton Moor. This furnace is thought to date from 1580 and was probably built by Huguenot glass workers, French Calvinist Protestants who fled to this remote corner of England at the time of the French Wars of Religion. It is thought that the furnace was abandoned around 1600, perhaps they had been discovered? The Elizabethan glass furnace was removed from Spaunton Moor and reconstructed at the Ryedale Folk Museum. The tradition of handmade glass continues today at the studio of Gillies Jones Glass, which can be found at Rosedale Abbey.

THE ROSEDALE IRONSTONE INDUSTRY flourished for seventy years during the late 19th Century turning this peaceful valley into an industrial landscape, for here was Yorkshire's very own 'Klondyke'. Ironstone had been mined here since the Iron Age, albeit on a very small scale, and later the monks of Byland Abbey and St Mary's at York established small bloomeries in the valley; however, all of this changed when a large seam of rich ironstone was discovered during the mid 19th Century. In 1856 the first mine opened above Hollins Farm just to the south of Rosedale Abbey, quickly followed by another mine near Thorgill in 1857 (later known as Sheriff's Pit); these mines were known as the West Mines as they were located on the west side of the valley. Around this time a rich seam of ironstone was discovered on the east side of Rosedale and so in 1860 the East Mines opened, followed in 1873 by a mine on the Farndale side of Blakey Ridge. The Industrial Revolution had arrived in Rosedale. The population of the valley rose six-fold in just two decades to almost 3,000, with probably the same number again lodging on a temporary basis in local houses. It is hard to imagine the ugly intrusive face of industry in what is now such a tranquil scene with terraces of miners' cottages, workshops, mine buildings, spoil heaps, noise, pollution and even a railway. Indeed, our route crosses the old cinder track-bed of this railway, one of the most remarkable railways in England.

Between 1856 and 1861 the ironstone was taken by horse-drawn wagons to the railway station at Pickering, a difficult and slow journey along poor roads. Due to the appalling condition of these roads, not to mention Rosedale's isolated location, a standard gauge railway was constructed in 1861 by the North Eastern Railway Company to transport ironstone from Rosedale to Teesside and coal from the Durham coalfields back to Rosedale to be used in the kilns. This amazing feat of engineering followed the contours of the hills perfectly for eleven miles from Bank Top above Rosedale Abbey, around the head of Farndale to Incline Top above Ingleby Greenhow from where loaded goods wagons were lowered down a 1-in-5 incline from the escarpment of the Cleveland Hills to join the main line at Battersby Junction. At Bank Top above Rosedale Abbey, a tramway incline was built to haul the ironstone up out of the valley from the mines near Hollins Farm to the railway terminus at Bank Top, whilst at Sheriff's Pit a vertical shaft was dug so that the ironstone could be hauled up almost 300-ft from the mines near Thorgill to the railway line above. In 1865 a branch line was built from Blakey Junction around the head of Rosedale to link up with the East Mines.

At its height during the 1870s over 300,000 tons of iron ore was transported by rail to Teesside annually, peaking at over 560,000 tons in 1873. However, these boom years did not last long. A slump in the markets coupled with cheaper imports meant that by 1885 the West Mines (Hollins Farm) had closed, followed by Blakey Mines in 1895, Sheriff's Pit in 1911, although the East Mines continued until the General Strike of 1926. Three years later the last train was lowered down the Incline and the Rosedale Ironstone Industry was over. The fascinating relics of this industry are all around to discover with rows of miners cottages that look oddly out of place, the old track-bed of the railway, spoil heaps and the stone arches of the calcining kilns at Bank Top and East Mines above Hill Cottages. These kilns were used to 'roast' the ironstone to reduce its weight before it was transported by train to Teesside, a process known as calcination. This not only lowered transport costs but also meant that less duty was paid on the ironstone!

ROSEDALE ABBEY may disappoint some visitors who come here in search of majestic ruins to rival those of Rievaulx. Little is left of the Cistercian Priory that gave the village its name, apart from a stone turret housing a spiral staircase, a sundial and several smaller fragments that have been incorporated into the neighbouring parish church. First established in 1158 this small priory, dedicated to St Mary and St Lawrence, was home to nine nuns and a prioress and remained a quiet place of worship until the Dissolution of the Monasteries in 1535. The Priory owned quite extensive tracts of land mainly to the south around Cawthorn and Lockton on which sheep were reared predominantly for their wool. The Priory buildings remained very much intact up until the middle of the 19th Century when almost all of the stone was plundered for building material during the boom of the ironstone mines. The Church of St Mary and St Lawrence dates from 1839 and stands on the site of the original Priory Church. Inside you will find two carved stones that possibly came from the cloisters (now the school playground), a stone seat and a gravestone inscribed with a cross and the name Maria, whilst outside there is a carved lintel above the north door with the words Omnia Vanitas (All is Vanity). The footpath through the large campsite passes a small stone building known as Waterhouse Well that provided the Priory with its drinking water inside which you will find a stone seat and a spout of crystal clear water. The Milburn Arms, much altered in the 18th and 19th centuries, originally belonged to the Priory when it was possibly used as the Steward's House. This pub was known as the Crown Inn during the mining days, changing its name to the Milburn Arms in 1958.

Almost all of the buildings in the village date from the heyday of the ironstone mines with attractive Victorian stone terraces crowding around a small central green. When the mines were in production Rosedale Abbey was home to numerous craftsmen and tradesmen, various shops, a water-mill and even a temporary hospital that was housed in the present school building! Even today, Rosedale Abbey appears to have a disproportionate number of inns and shops for such a small village. A narrow road leads out of the village up past the White Horse Farm Inn to reach Bank Top from where motorists are treated to wonderful views of Rosedale. This is Chimney Bank, one of the steepest roads in the country with 1-in-3 inclines and hairpin bends, although some of the bends look almost vertical! *"Look at those savage cliff-like roads that sweep down to Grosmont from Sleights Moor or from Egton across the valley, or at Rosedale Chimney. They are stupendous, with gradients of about 1 in 3 or 4, and as you walk down to the valley from the ridge you seem to be descending to the bowels of the earth, but just when you think you have got down the steepest bit, the land falls away again and the road takes another terrific lunge down the next drop; and so it goes on."* **(A. J. Brown 'Broad Acres' 1948)**. The 'chimney' from which the road takes its name relates to the engine-house chimney of the West Mines that once stood at Bank Top, a famous landmark visible for miles around until it was demolished in 1972 because no money could be found to repair it. The chimney need not have been so high, but was built to a height of 100-feet on the insistence of a local landowner who did not want the smoke to upset his grouse!

Lealholm

STAGE FIVE

. . . .

ROSEDALE ABBEY
to
HAWNBY

✦

"We turned off the narrow road along an old track that was to take us out of Farndale up towards the bulk of Rudland Rigg; our objective, Bransdale. For centuries before us, countless travellers, tradesmen and drovers have walked this way, and here we were continuing this tradition of travelling on foot, albeit it with leather boots, rucksacks and maps. Near some crags, we stopped for a rest on a grassy ledge, a respite from the climb and a chance to admire the view. We took off our rucksacks, searched for our water bottles then relaxed in the morning sunshine, with upper Farndale laid out before us in all of its glory. This was the life, we thought, and a whole day of moorland walking ahead of us. At that moment, an almighty crack of thunder shook the ground we lay on. We looked behind to find a menacing sheet of dark grey clouds where blue sky had been minutes before. With a wall of rain fast approaching, we just managed to zip up our jackets before a Biblical storm was upon us. Without warning hailstones the size of marbles, and nearly as hard, were pelting us, our faces red raw and stinging. The rough track was now a raging river of orange brown water. We both looked at each other and laughed. A whole day of moorland walking ahead of us!"

Mark Reid
June 2000

WALK INFORMATION

Points of interest: Secluded valleys and heather-clad ridges, wild daffodils, an old Corpse Way, the mill built by a multi-lingual Reverend, 16th Century thatched Spout House, England's most unusual cricket pitch and the Tale of Two Villages.

Distance:
Rosedale Abbey to Church Houses	4 miles
Church Houses to Spout House	8 miles
Spout House to Hawnby	4 miles
Total	16 miles

Time: Allow 8 hours

Terrain: This walk predominantly follows clear moorland tracks and paths. However, the sections from Thorgill up onto Blakey Ridge, from Bonfield Gill up across Bilsdale East Moor as well as the descent into Farndale and Bonfield Gill follow narrow paths across open moorland with rough/boggy terrain; some of the paths are indistinct in places - care must be taken in poor weather. This walk crosses five moorland ridges - Blakey Ridge, Rudland Rigg, Bransdale Ridge, Bilsdale East Moor and the high ground to the north of Easterside Hill. Some of the ascents are long and quite strenuous, although the paths/tracks are clearly defined for most of the way. There are some short sections of road walking through the valleys, mostly along quiet country lanes.

This walk crosses five moorland ridges, some sections of which are remote and exposed to the elements with rough/boggy terrain and indistinct paths in places. Navigation may be difficult in poor weather - take

OS map and compass. The stream crossing over Bonfield Gill and ford over Ladhill Beck (near Hawnby) may be difficult after heavy rain. Take care walking alongside the B1257 road through Bilsdale.

Open Access	The short section along the shooters' track across Bilsdale East Moor (SE 585 945 to SE 583 943) is a permissive path across Open Access land. **www.openaccess.gov.uk**

Ascents:

Blakey Ridge:	356 metres
Rudland Rigg:	375 metres
Bransdale Ridge:	363 metres
Bilsdale East Moor:	343 metres
(north of) Easterside Hill:	244 metres

Viewpoints:
View across Rosedale from Sheriff's Pit.
Superb panorama of Farndale from Low Blakey Moor and along the track from Monket House up out of the valley.
Bransdale is seen to excellent effect during the descent from Rudland Rigg.
Stunning moorland scenery around Bonfield Gill.
Descent towards the Spout House (Sun Inn) offers wonderful views across Bilsdale.

FACILITIES

. . . .

Rosedale Abbey	Inn / B&B / Shop / Café / Bus / Phone / Toilets / Camp
Church Houses	Inn / Café / Phone
Spout House	Inn / Bus
Hawnby	Inn / B&B / Shop / Café / Phone

ROUTE DESCRIPTION

(Map Thirteen)

From the small 'green' in the centre of Rosedale Abbey, walk along the road into the heart of the village passing the church and the school on your right (passing between the school and the Abbey Stores) then, immediately after the school, take the road turning to the right. Follow this road curving round to the right for 100 yards then, as you become parallel with the scant priory ruins (stone staircase) and west end of the church across to your right, take the FP to the left that leads over a small stream and through a kissing-gate (SP 'Thorgill') into the campsite. After the kissing-gate, walk straight on over the campsite road and along a tree-lined grassy path and follow this curving slightly to the right after a short distance then straight on across the middle of the campsite to reach a FB across the River Seven in the far corner of the field. Cross the FB and head up some steps and through a small gate that leads out onto a field, then follow the paved path up across the field to reach the road through a gate (SE 719 958). Turn right along the road and follow this for almost 0.5 miles (passing Hobb Farm and then Thorgill House) then take the FP to the left over a ladder stile (SP). After the ladder stile, walk up through the gate in the wall just ahead to your right then bear slightly to the right across the field (walking along the foot of the sparsely wooded bank) through another gate at the top of the stone wall, after which continue straight on along a path which soon becomes a walled grassy track that leads down to join a track adjacent to the road at Thorgill (SE 709 964).

Turn left along the track *(do not head along road)* bearing left at the houses then, after a short distance, take the FP to the left by the last house that leads up through trees to soon reach a small gate, with a small ravine down to your right. After the small gate, continue up along the path and follow it curving round to the right (alongside this small ravine) to soon reach a fork in the path (at the head of this small ravine), where you follow the right-hand path that leads straight on alongside a stone wall on your right to reach a stile across your path. Cross the stile and continue straight up along what is now a walled grassy track (wall still on your right) to reach another stile by a small stream across your path, after which continue heading up the hillside (indistinct path) alongside the stone wall on your right. Where the wall turns down to the right, continue straight on heading up into the small valley (Thorgill Beck) gradually bearing to the right through bracken and heather and drop down to cross the stream over a small FB after the stone wall has ended on the right (upper reaches of Thorgill Beck - SE 703 959). Cross the FB and head straight up along a narrow path climbing quite steeply up out of the valley at first (wall just across to your right), then rising gently up along a narrow path that bears gradually to the left away from the wall up across the heather moorland then, where this wall turns away to the right after a fairly short distance, carry on along the narrow path up across the gently rising heather moorland bearing very slightly left to reach the old railway track-bed at the conspicuous ruins of Sheriff's Pit (SE 698 962).

Cross the cinder track-bed and follow the path opposite passing to the right-hand side of the ruined gable end of a house up onto the heather moorland of Blakey Ridge (cairns). The path gradually bears to the right across the moor for 0.3 miles to reach Pike Howe *(Bronze Age burial mound)* surmounted by a large cairn, after which continue straight on to reach the unenclosed moorland road across Blakey Ridge (SE 689 962). As you reach the road, turn right for approx. 25 yards and take the FP to the left (SP) then bear diagonally to the right down across the open heather moorland *(no clear path)* heading in a north-westerly direction (towards the upper reaches of Farndale in the distance) to soon reach a clear path along the top of a small ridge/steep slope overlooking Farndale. Follow this path to the right along the top of this small ridge then drop down to the left to pass through the corner of a tumbledown wall, after which continue straight on along the narrow path to quickly reach a small stream and then a drainage ditch after which continue on to soon reach the corner of a stone wall (SE 682 966). Head straight on with the wall on your left to reach a ladder stile over the wall, cross the ladder stile and head straight on with the wall on your left for approx. 100 yards then, adjacent to the gate on the left, turn right away from the wall along a sunken path that leads down to the road (SE 676 970).

(Map Fourteen)

Turn right along the road to quickly reach a road junction where you bear to the left (road sign 'Church Houses') and follow this road down into Church Houses. Follow the road through the hamlet, bending left around the pub (road sign 'Farndale West Side') and round to the right *(ignore lane off to the left)* out of the hamlet then follow this road straight on down to reach Thorn Wath Bridge across the River Dove and then quite steeply up to a road junction. Turn right at this road junction (road sign 'Dale End, West Only') for 175 yards then take the track to the left through a gate immediately after Monket House, marked by a SP 'Bransdale' (SE 660 972). Follow this rough track steeply up passing through spoil heaps *(ignore track turning off to the left by the old railings)* for 0.5 miles up onto the moor. As you reach the top of the moor the track levels out, continue on along the track for a further 0.75 miles to reach the 'crossroads' with the clearer track across the top of Rudland Rigg (Westside Road). Walk straight on at the 'crossroads' continuing along the same track and follow this for just over a mile across the broad moorland ridge (Rudland Rigg) then down into Bransdale to reach the road at Cow Sike Farm (SE 625 981).

(Map Fifteen)

At the road, turn right then head left over a stile immediately after the farm buildings. Cross the first small field down over another stile then bear slightly to the left down the hillside to pass through the left-hand gate of two gates. After this gate, continue down alongside the fence on your right and through another gate *(the right–hand gate of two gates)* as you reach the bottom of this field, then head down across the next field (keeping close to the wall on your left) to reach a small gate near a telegraph pole that leads down to Bransdale Mill via stone steps (SE 621 979). At Bransdale Mill, cross the stone bridge over Hodge Beck and head through the gate between the barns and follow the path up passing a stone sundial then straight up across the field to reach a gate in the wall at the top of the field, after which carry straight on heading up across the field and through another gate towards the top left corner of the field *(Colt House Farm ahead of you)*. Head though this gate and walk up towards Colt House Farm then, as you approach the farm buildings, head up across the field to reach a gate to the right of the farm buildings in the top corner of the field that leads onto a road at a sharp bend, marked by a SP (SE 616 975).

Cross the road and head through the gate opposite to the right (SP) along a wide, rough walled track that leads up to join another road. Turn left and follow this road for 0.75 miles climbing up to the top of Bransdale Ridge. Where the road levels out at the top of the ridge continue along the road for a short distance passing a track on the right (metal barrier) just after which take the FP bearing off to the right, marked by a SP (SE 609 962). Follow this narrow path to soon reach a boundary stone (inscribed with 'K' & 'H') where you continue along the narrow path for almost 0.5 miles across heather moorland gradually bearing left down into the valley of Bonfield Gill to reach the corner of a stone wall. Head down with the wall on your left into the bottom of the valley (boggy ground), over the stream of Bonfield Gill (ford) then straight up the hillside keeping close to the wall and small plantation on your left to quickly reach a shooters' track across your path (SE 601 953). Cross over the track and follow the narrow path (cairn) up through the heather marked by a series of small cairns gradually bearing to the left up across the broad ridge of Bilsdale East Moor. As you head up onto the top of the broad moorland ridge, the path straightens out and meanders across the top of the moor before it begins its gradual descent, bearing slightly left again, to reach a shooting track across your path after 0.75 miles (SE 591 948). Head straight over this track and follow the narrow path *(indistinct in places)* bearing very slightly to the left across the heather moorland (marked by small cairns) heading in a south-westerly direction for approx. 250 yards to join an overgrown/heather-covered sunken path (bridleway), where you carry straight on alongside this sunken path on your left gently dropping down to reach another shooters' track across your path (SE 585 945). Turn left along this track *(permissive path*)* and follow it down to join a stone wall/fence on your right (track now becomes a path). Head left alongside this fence for approx. 300 yards *(ignore stile over the fence to the right)* then, as the fence ends and stone wall bends away to the right, continue straight on along the clear path *(Public Footpath)* which gradually slants down across the hillside. The path passes a corner of a stone wall and continues straight on gradually slanting down across the hillside (wall just down to your right) for 0.25 miles down to reach two gates set in the bottom corner of the wall (SE 579 936). Head through the left-hand gate *(ignore gate to the right)* and follow the grassy track down to another gate in a fence (just beside the corner of Spout House Plantation on your left), after which head down the field to the right, over a stile in the fence and down across another field then through the farmyard to reach the Sun Inn (Spout House) and the road.

* Our route from the shooters' track at SE 585 945 to the Public Footpath at SE 583 943 is a permissive path across Open Access land.

(Map Sixteen)

Turn left along the road *(take care)* for approx. 0.25 miles then take the track to the right (SP) down towards Helm House, over a bridge across the River Seph after which head off to the left through a gate by a telegraph pole (as the track bends away up to the right) that leads out onto a field. After the gate, head straight up across the field alongside the fence/hedge on your right through two gates at the top of the field between some barns, after which turn left behind the barns through a wooden gate along an enclosed grassy track (SE 567 933). Follow the clear track straight on through two more gates after which the track becomes unenclosed and less distinct; however, continue straight on alongside a fence/wall on your left until you reach a stone wall across your path in the bottom corner of the field (at the end of the field). As you reach the wall in the bottom corner of the field, head up to the right alongside the wall on your left to reach a gate in this wall/fence on your left (three-quarters of the way up the field). Go through the gate and continue straight on across the next field alongside the wall on your left, through another gate after which follow the indistinct grassy track bearing slightly to the right up across the field to reach a gate that leads into a plantation. Follow the track up through the woods then, as you emerge from the woods, continue along the walled, grassy track for 0.25 miles to join a road. Cross over the road and follow the track opposite up to reach Low Ewe Cote Farm (SE 561 918).

Walk straight on through the farmyard (passing the back of the farmhouse on your left) then follow the track round to the right after the farm buildings up to reach a gate at the start of a walled, grassy track. Follow this walled track up for approx. 150 yards then, after the next gate (walled track ends), bear right through another gate after which head to the left up across the field (alongside the wall on your left) to reach a gate in the top left-hand corner of the field (moorland ahead). After the gate, head straight on along the sunken path directly ahead. This sunken path quickly divides - follow the left-hand branch along the bottom of the left-hand sunken pathway *(ignore moorland path between the two sunken paths)*, which quickly becomes a clear, narrow path that gradually bears to the left across the heather moorland for 0.25 miles to reach a gate in a stone wall in the shadow of Easterside Hill (SE 552 915).

Head through the gate and walk straight on across the rough grassy moorland, with the fence to your right, along a path that soon becomes a rough track. Follow this track straight on alongside the fence on your right for approx. 0.25 miles then head to the right through a gate in this fence, after which head left along the track towards High Banniscue Farm for a short distance then, as you approach the farm, head left through a bridlegate (SP). After the bridlegate, head up to the right to quickly reach another bridlegate then head straight on across the field along an indistinct track skirting to the left above the farm buildings to join a clear track just after the farm buildings. Head straight on (to the left) along this track (away from the farm buildings) and follow this track for 0.75 miles passing through Banniscue Wood all the way to reach the road (SE 551 899). At the road turn right and follow the road steeply down over a ford (Ladhill Beck) then steeply up into Hawnby.

Sun Inn, Bilsdale

MAP THIRTEEN

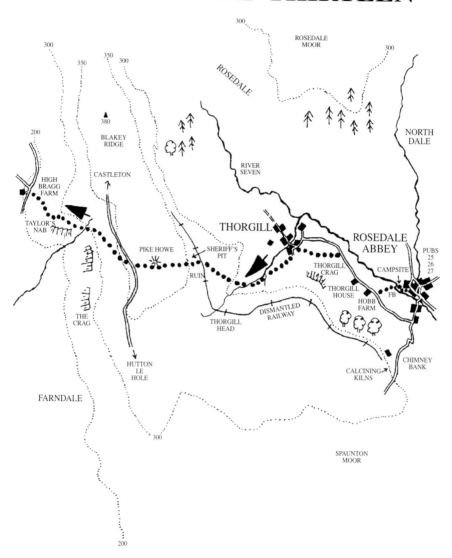

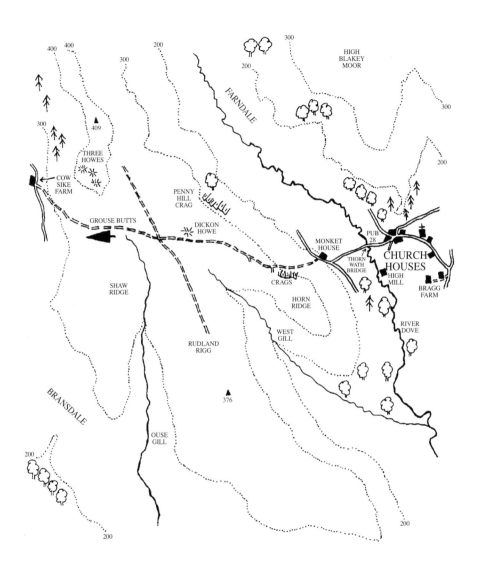

MAP FOURTEEN

MAP FIFTEEN

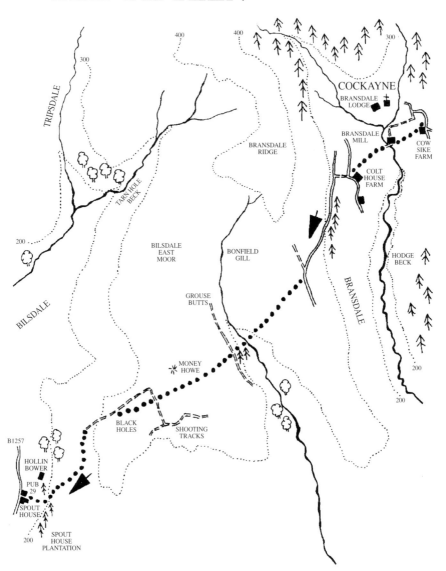

167

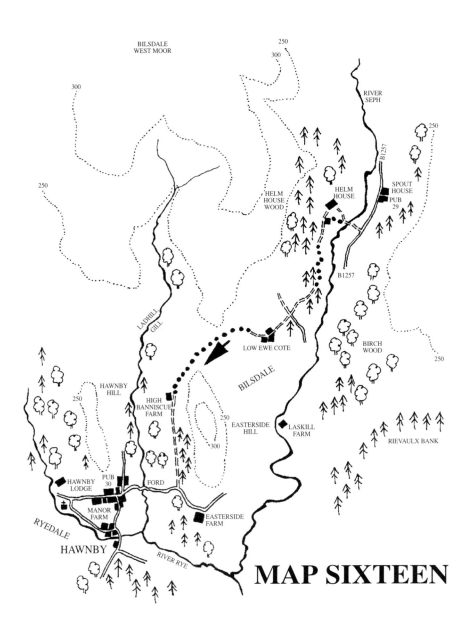

BILSDALE
WEST MOOR

250

300

300

RIVER
SEPH

250

250

HELM
HOUSE
WOOD

HELM
HOUSE

B1257

SPOUT
HOUSE
PUB
29

B1257

LADHILL GILL

LOW EWE COTE

BILSDALE

BIRCH
WOOD

250

HAWNBY
HILL

250

HIGH
BANNISCUE
FARM

250

EASTERSIDE
HILL

LASKILL
FARM

RIEVAULX BANK

300

HAWNBY
LODGE

PUB
30

FORD

MANOR
FARM

EASTERSIDE
FARM

RYEDALE

HAWNBY

RIVER RYE

MAP SIXTEEN

SHERIFF'S PIT is the name given to the huge shaft that was excavated in 1857 to provide a quick and easy way of transporting the ironstone from the West Mines up to the railway line on the flanks of Blakey Ridge. The shaft plunges 270-feet to link up with a 1,500-ft long level that was cut into the side of the hill near to the West Mines at Thorgill. Winding gear similar to that of an old coal mine once stood above the shaft with workshops, stores and the Mines Manager's House nearby. The West Mines closed completely in 1911 and the buildings were subsequently pulled down; all that remains are the ruins of the Managers' House and the foundations of the workshops. Water now trickles down into the dark chasm of Sheriff's Pit, which is protected by safety fencing. The Pit was named after Alexander Sheriff, one of the owners of the Rosedale and Ferryhill Mining Co that operated the mines until 1879.

BLAKEY RIDGE separates Farndale and Rosedale, a high shoulder of land that provides one of the few routes through the heart of the North York Moors from Hutton-le-Hole in the south to Castleton in the north. This road has been in constant use for centuries and may date back to prehistoric times as the surrounding moors are littered with Bronze and Iron Age remains. In medieval times monks travelled this way and later the road was used by drovers, packhorses and as a coach road; it was metalled in 1932 and still provides an exhilarating high-level motor road over the moors. Alongside the road are many reminders of travellers of centuries past with old stone crosses and guideposts dotted along the route. Near the highest point stand two of the most famous crosses of the North York Moors. Young Ralph Cross stands tall and proud, the emblem of the North York Moors National Park, whilst close by is Old Ralph Cross, a photograph of which graces the front cover of this book. There has been a cross on this high moorland since at least 1200 when a 'Crux Radulph' was mentioned as being on Westerdale Moor, although the present stone Old Ralph Cross dates from the 18th Century. Just to the south of these crosses stands the solitary Lion Inn, the highest pub on the moors that is said to date back to the 16th Century although some claim it was built as a monastic hostelry in the 14th Century.

FARNDALE is perhaps the most famous valley in the North York Moors for one reason; it is the valley of the daffodils. But there is so much more to Farndale than these attractive yellow flowers. Coal and ironstone has been worked on the surrounding moors for centuries, however, these workings were on a much smaller scale than neighbouring Rosedale and therefore Farndale has less scars to heal. The upper reaches of Farndale above Church Houses remain beautifully unspoilt with sturdy stone farmsteads set at regular intervals along the West Side and East Side roads that lead into this unfrequented corner of the North York Moors; both roads are dead-ends. Unlike the Yorkshire Dales, many of the dales of the North York Moors are not named after the rivers that flow through them, and Farndale is no exception. The River Dove flows leisurely through the meadows and pastures, its banks thickly wooded with deciduous trees, indeed 'Farndale' comes from the old Celtic word for 'alder trees' as in prehistoric times much of the valley floor would have been swamp, whilst 'dove' comes from the Celtic word for 'black' possibly due to the peaty water. *"...the little River Dove seems to dance down the dale as to a piper's tune; past the hamlet of Church Houses (with its comfortable Feversham Arms) down to the picturesque village of Low Mill in the middle, its banks bordered by pleasant farms, green pastures and fair woods."* **(A. J. Brown 'Fair North Riding' 1952).**

Farndale is famed throughout the country for its display of wild spring daffodils (known locally as Lenten Lilies as they bloom around Easter) that carpet the fields and riverbanks, the damp valley bottom providing a perfect habitat for these flowers. A short circular walk from Low Mill to Church Houses alongside the River Dove is a very popular walk in spring when the daffodils are at their best, but pick your times carefully as the car parks soon fill up and special buses are laid on from Hutton-le-Hole to bring crowds of people to see the daffodils, although they spend most of their time queuing to climb stiles! In 1953 2,000 acres of Farndale was designated a Nature Reserve due to the threat to the daffodils from visitors who thought that the flowers would look better in a vase on their mantelpiece rather than in their natural setting; it is an offence to pick them! There are many stories as to how these daffodils came to be in this valley, some say that they were planted by the monks of Rievaulx or by the community of Friars who settled in the valley during the Middle Ages or even by Father Postgate, who is said to have given them the name of Lenten Lilies. Even more unbelievable is the fact that the upper reaches of the valley above Church Houses were very nearly flooded as part of a huge reservoir scheme to provide the thirsty city of Hull with drinking water. The idea first surfaced in the 1930s and again reared its ugly head in the late 1960s when the plan was eventually thrown out by a Select Committee of the House of Commons after a fierce battle. How could they even think of flooding this beautiful valley? *"It seems unbelievable, as you walk along and look down at the tranquil loveliness of Farndale, that there are men with souls so dead, with visions so clouded, with appreciation of natural beauty so withered, that they actually scheme to flood the valley with water permanently. You simply can't credit it, can you?"* **(A. Wainwright 'A Coast to Coast Walk' 1973)**.

Of all the stories about hobgoblins throughout the North York Moors, Farndale's Hob is perhaps the most famous. For generations the Farndale Hob had helped a local farming family with chores around the farm, working in secret for his nightly jug of cream. Over the years the farm grew prosperous; however, the farmer's wife died young and he remarried, but his new wife was a bit of a penny pincher and decided to replace the cream with skimmed milk! The Hob suddenly became very mischievous and soon the fortunes of the farm took a turn for the worse. Life for this unfortunate farmer and his wife became so unbearable that they decided to pack up and leave and so loaded all of their possessions onto his horse and cart and set off. One of his neighbours spotted him and asked where he was going, the farmer explained his predicament and said that they were leaving the farm for good (or 'flitting' in local dialect) at which point a voice came from his cart *"Aye, we're flittin!"* Resigned to the fact that the Farndale Hob was never going to leave him, the farmer turned his cart round and headed home. On the moors to the east of Farndale is a plundered burial mound known as Obtrusch Roque, which is said to be the home of the Farndale Hobgoblin. *"As regards Obtrush Roque one cannot do better than refer to Professor Phillips, who, with some friends, excavated it in 1836. He speaks of it as a 'goblin-haunted mound'..."* (**J. S. Fletcher 'Nooks and Corners of Yorkshire').**

CHURCH HOUSES is a tiny hamlet consisting of one or two cottages, a farm, village hall, church and one of the most remote pubs in the North York Moors. The road through the hamlet appears more like someone's front yard rather than a through-road. It is a sleepy place for eleven months of the year; however, when the daffodils are in bloom the hamlet becomes thronged with visitors. Just outside the hamlet hidden amongst trees is the Church of St Mary, which dates from 1831 when a chapel was built to serve the valley, although the church was extensively rebuilt in 1871 with the help of Lord Feversham after Bransdale and Farndale became two separate parishes. This site may have been used for worship since the Middle Ages as a community of Friars, known as the Little Brothers of The Trinity, established a house in Farndale in the 14th Century.

THORN WATH BRIDGE is a simple stone bridge across the River Dove to the west of Church Houses, which has been a fording point for centuries as 'wath' is the old word for 'ford'. Some say that this was also the setting for Farndale's very own 'Romeo and Juliet' story, that of Sarkless Kitty. Kitty Garthwaite was a pretty Farndale girl who fell in love with the son of a wealthy farmer. They were due to be wed, however, when she told him that she was pregnant he turned his back on her. She begged him to change his mind and eventually he agreed to meet Kitty to talk things through, only he did not turn up for their secret rendezvous. She went to find him but found the river to be in full spate and so assumed that he could not cross the ford to meet her, but as she was leaving a local man saw the distressed Kitty and told her that he had seen her lover riding off down the valley. Overcome with grief, Kitty took off her clothes (hence 'sarkless') and threw herself into the raging river and drowned. When they found her body it had been washed up on the riverbank at Lowna next to the body of her lover. He had apparently gone to

Kirkbymoorside to buy her a wedding ring and on his return had been swept away by the river and he too had drowned. Local people believed that they had killed themselves and so buried them next to the ford instead of consecrated ground, however, a ghostly apparition of a naked woman was often seen near this spot and several other people also drowned in the river so the bodies were exhumed and buried in a local graveyard.

RUDLAND RIGG is a huge ridge of moorland that extends almost the entire length of the North York Moors from Kirkbymoorside in the south to the escarpment of the Cleveland Hills above Ingleby Greenhow, with the beautiful valleys of Bransdale to the west and Farndale to the east. An old coach road, known as Waingate (meaning 'wagon road') in medieval times, follows the high ground along the top of Rudland Rigg. This old road is still a rough track for most of the way providing an exhilarating walk high above the neighbouring valleys with the endless moors stretching away in every direction; you really do feel as though you are 'away from it all' whilst walking across Rudland Rigg. *"Oh, the feeling of freshness and freedom up there, with the air keen and the wind sharp, but carrying with it, in the season, the scent of heather. I often feel that the soul of the North York Moors lies in and around Rudland Rigg because the motif of the whole area is distance and heather."* **(J. Herriot 'James Herriot's Yorkshire' 1979)**. All around are relics from the past including Bronze Age burial mounds, old guideposts with strange phonetic spellings such as 'kirby rode' and long abandoned coal pits. Our route up over the ridge leaves Farndale near Monket House and climbs steeply beneath Monket House Crags then crosses the Rudland Rigg road and continues on passing just south of Three Howes (Bronze Age burial mounds) and then down into Bransdale. This track was known as Munckgate in the Middle Ages and was used by the people of Farndale as a route to the churchyard at Cockayne in Bransdale before the churchyard at Church Houses was consecrated; this is one of the few 'Corpse Ways' in the North York Moors.

BRANSDALE gradually unfolds before your eyes as you drop down along the old track from Rudland Rigg, a beautiful pastoral scene across the broad green valley scattered with stone farmhouses and copses of trees. These farmhouses, built from local stone and red pantiles (or roof tiles), are stout and sturdy yet blend perfectly with their surroundings, they also have very colourful names such as Toad Hole, Cow Sike, Yoad House and Spout House. Bransdale, named after a Viking settler called Brand, is the name given to the upper reaches of the valley from the dale head amongst the highest hills of the North York Moors at Round Hill (454 metres above sea level) until the valley narrows into a deep ravine near Ankness Farm, a distance of about four miles, from where the valley is known as Sleightholme Dale and then Kirkdale; only the name of the small river that flows through this valley keeps its name all of the way, that of Hodge Beck. Bransdale is the most remote valley in the North York Moors with two narrow unfenced roads leading into it and no villages or tourist attractions to draw the crowds. *The very fact, however, that those things which appeal to a certain type of tourist are missing from some of the minor dales of which I am about to write, is no drawback to some "with an eye for a country", and heart attuned. There are no "road houses" in my daleland, no up-to-date hotels, indeed, no artificial veneer. Each dale is unspoilt, little touched by modernism, and peopled by a rough-hewn clan, full of character, living apart, and in a very real sense fitting into the weft and warp of their surroundings.* **(J. & R. Fairfax-Blakeborough 'The Spirit of Yorkshire' 1954).** The only settlement in Bransdale is called Cockayne, although in reality this is little more than a rather grand shooting lodge, a cottage or two and a simple church. The Church of St Nicholas was rebuilt in 1886 on the site of a much earlier chapel. The church is noted for its Norman font, striking ceiling and breathtaking views along the length of the dale from the churchyard. Bransdale is thankfully in the care of the National Trust and so will remain an oasis of tranquillity forever.

BRANSDALE MILL is one of the oldest mills in the North York Moors dating back to at least the 13th Century. This old mill ground corn and, unusually, oatmeal, for local farmers until the 1930s, an essential amenity in days gone by hence the number of paths and tracks that converge on it. William Strickland restored Bransdale Mill during the early 19th Century; a stone tablet proclaims the date of 1842 as the year it was finished. William was assisted by his son Emmanuel who was the vicar of Ingleby Greenhow, a well educated man who obviously wanted the world to know this fact by erecting a stone tablet inscribed with Greek, Latin and Hebrew text, not to mention a long list of letters after his name! The resulting mill complex stands as a rather extensive industrial complex for such a remote place and is a fascinating place to explore with its many out-buildings, stone bridge, mill-race and sundial. It is in the care of the National Trust who have recently restored it.

From Bransdale our route heads west over Bransdale Ridge and then across the wild and lonely moorland of Bilsdale East Moor via the hidden valley of Bonfield Gill, a little-known tributary of the River Riccal. This wonderful heather moorland is certainly 'away from it all', the preserve of grouse, lapwings, curlews and skylarks with shooters' tracks stretching into the horizon like yellow ribbons laid across the gently rising moors.

BILSDALE was known as Smiddesdale until 1145, an Old Norse name meaning 'smithies valley' derived from the many primitive ironstone bloomeries (or furnaces) that were operating in the valley well over 1,000 years ago. It was in that year that Walter Espec of Helmsley Castle gave the monks of Rievaulx Abbey vast tracts of land in the valley. The name of Bilsdale is most probably named after a Scandinavian settler called Bild; however, some accounts claim that William the Conqueror travelled through the valley after his terrible Harrying of the North in the 11th Century, hence 'Bill's Dale', although this is a rather fanciful story as he almost certainly travelled along Hambleton Street several miles to the west. From the natural 'saddle' of land on the escarpment of the Cleveland Hills between Urra Moor and Hasty Bank, the diminutive Bilsdale Beck flows south to join with the waters of Raisdale Beck at Chop Gate to form the River Seph. This river then continues through the broad, lush acres of Bilsdale generously cloaked with ancient oaks until it merges with the River Rye in the shadow of Easterside Hill. There are no large villages, only a scattering of small hamlets with musical names: Urra,

Chop Gate (pronounced 'Chop Yat') and Fangdale Beck. Many of the farms in the valley were established by the monks of Rievaulx as monastic farms or 'granges'; the main granges were at Laskill, Newlass and Griff, however a glance at the map will reveal many farm names that have strong links with the monks such as Low Ewe Cote, Woolhouse Croft and Cross Holme Farm. Towering above the east side of the valley to a height of around 1,000-feet is the Bilsdale Television Mast, a major landmark visible for miles throughout the North York Moors National Park and beyond, an amazing sight indeed when inspected from close quarters.

THE SPOUT HOUSE is one of the most fascinating buildings in the country and possibly the oldest house in the North York Moors still in its original location. This cruck-framed cottage was built in 1550 and was originally a farm tenant's dwelling becoming a licensed inn in 1714, although it is likely to have provided refreshment and shelter for travellers for many years before the farmer obtained a formal beer license. For 200 years the Spout House (also known as the Sun Inn) quenched the thirst of local farmers and travellers before it closed its doors in 1914 when the present-day Sun Inn was built across the yard. Time literally stood still within this old pub until the 1970s when the National Park Committee stepped in to restore the building as it was fast falling down. Many of the original fixtures and fittings remain including very rare beds fitted into the attic known as 'truckle beds', period furniture and wooden beer barrels in a cool cellar. The Spout House remains completely unaltered and offers a unique insight into how country inns used to be centuries ago. The name of 'Spout House' can be found throughout the North York Moors and usually relates to a nearby spring or well. *"The building is used as an outhouse now, but it is easy to imagine the cosy atmosphere of its large main room and the groups sitting round the fireplace, for here again the turf fire is kept continually burning, and much of the cooking for the new inn is done on it. Times have changed, but the topics of the farmers who gather at Spout House now are still corn and cows and markets, and life and death in the dale."* **(E. Pontefract & M. Hartley 'Yorkshire Tour' 1939).**

The 'new' Sun Inn is a classic example of an old fashioned country pub with several small rooms and unpretentious surroundings. The landlord of the Sun Inn has been a William Ainsley since 1823; the current William Ainsley is a farmer as well as an innkeeper thus continuing a tradition that stretches back centuries. A story is told of two visitors who came into the pub one rainy night and began playing dominoes to pass the time, however, they were playing without a set of dominoes. For a good hour or so they held up their imaginary dominoes concentrating on their next move. When the game had finished one of the men got up to refill his glass of beer and asked the landlord if he had any darts, *"They're stuck in the board"* he said pointing at the bare dartboard, *"you've managed all night with your dominoes, now have a go at darts!"* The Sun Inn has strong associations with the Bilsdale Hunt, one of the oldest hunts in the country, which regularly meets outside the pub. To the right of the front door is the gravestone of Bobbie Dowson, a famous local huntsman ('whip to the Bilsdale Hounds for upwards of 60 years') as well as cricketer of the Spout House team who died in 1902. The local vicar refused to have this headstone in his churchyard because of the hunting motifs carved onto it, so it was erected outside Bobby's favourite pub instead! If you look at the hillside behind the pub you may also spot the flat wicket of a cricket pitch cut into an otherwise steep and rough hillside. The long established Spout House Cricket Team certainly boasts one of the most unusual pitches in the country that makes for an interesting game of cricket.

HAWNBY, named after a Scandinavian farmer called Halmi, lies hidden amongst the hills of upper Ryedale, a picturesque cluster of honey-coloured stone cottages built somewhat confusingly at the top and the foot of a long, steep hill - it is a village of two halves. A story is told of two local men who were working out on the moors one sunny day during the mid 18th Century when they decided to take a nap. To their amazement they both had the same dream that God himself had spoken to them to change their ways and convert. They walked back down to Hawnby and noticed a newspaper article about John Wesley who was due to preach at Newcastle - it was a sign! So they set off on foot and walked all the way up to Newcastle and returned as converts to the 'new' Methodist faith. But things were to take a turn for the worse as they were subsequently evicted from their homes in 'high' Hawnby when Lord Tancred, a staunch Protestant, found out. They set up home at the foot of the hill in what is today 'lower' Hawnby, ever since when the village has been a stronghold of Methodism. Indeed John Wesley came to the village in 1757 and later wrote eloquently about this village with its large Methodist community as well as his journey across the moors between Osmotherley and Hawnby. Look out for the old Wesleyan Chapel dated 1770 tucked away near to the village shop complete with old pulpit, pot-bellied stove and tiered pews. Close by, Hawnby Bridge spans the River Rye, an elegant stone structure that was designed by the famous architect John Carr who also designed Harewood House and Buxton's Crescent, although his 'bread and butter' was bridges.

Away from the village, hidden in trees on the banks of the River Rye stands the 12th Century All Saints Church, a plain and simple place of worship set in tranquil surroundings. This fascinating church has a stained glass window with scenes from the Great War as well as a long list of local men who lost their lives during the First World War, a surprising number considering the size of Hawnby. This is due to the fact that the vicar of the time was known as the 'fighting parson of Hawnby' who encouraged the local men to join up - not such a good idea looking at the number of names on the memorial. The church was rebuilt in the 14th Century as it is said to have been ransacked by the army of Robert the Bruce in 1322 when he came this way in pursuit of Edward II's army. It is also the last resting-place for generations of the Tancred family who once lived at nearby Arden Hall.

The hills that shelter Hawnby form part of the Tabular Hills, an extensive range of predominantly limestone hills dissected by countless deep valleys that run along the southern boundary of the North York Moors rising gently from the Vale of Pickering before dropping steeply away towards the central heather moors. The distinctive profiles of Hawnby Hill and Easterside Hill dominate the scene, their bright green grassy slopes stand out against the harsher heather moors that lap at their feet to the north. *"The dales that stretch away in various directions from Rievaulx are as lonely as they are picturesque. In summer they are solitary; in winter, almost impossible to traverse. One may follow such roads or paths as there are along them for considerable distances without encountering a human being or seeing more than an occasional farmstead, far away from the world. But of their beauty no one will doubt who cares to explore their recesses."* **(J. S. Fletcher 'The Enchanting North' 1908).**

Hawnby

HAWNBY
to
HELMSLEY

✦

"Far horizons of hazy heather moorland with Hawnby Hill,
Easterside Hill, Rievaulx Bank and Birk Nab showing their
characteristic 'tabular' shape to good effect, lined up into the distance
gently rising yet steeply falling away towards the moors as if ready to
pounce. Beneath my feet a dizzy drop into deep, lush valleys cloaked
in ancient oak woodland and scattered here and there diminutive
honey-coloured farmsteads sleeping amongst the pastures. My only
companions are the sounds of curlew, sheep and a farm collie drifting
with the warm breeze. I look down to my path-scarred boots pointing
over the edge of Noddle End ridge... what a pleasure it is to be
here on the high ground above Ryedale."

Mark Reid
July 2000

WALK INFORMATION

Points of interest:	Table-top mountains, a hidden nunnery, primeval oak forests, ancient drovers' roads, a Celtic hill fort, the finest view in England, the stinging valley and the magnificent monastic ruins of 'Rye Vale'.

Distance:

Hawnby to Scawton	10 miles
Scawton to Helmsley	6 miles
Total	16 miles

Time: Allow 7 hours

Terrain:

This walk follows well defined stony/grassy tracks, several field paths, a short section across moorland and a long stretch along a grassy path that follows the crest of the Hambleton Hills escarpment. There are also several short sections along quiet country lanes. The ascent from Arden Hall to Dale Town Common is long and quite steep in places along a clear track, and there are several wooded valleys along the way with short but quite steep descents and ascents including Flassen Dale, Nettle Dale, Low Gill and Ryedale. The section along the top of the Hambleton escarpment, especially along Boltby Scar, is exposed to the elements with cliffs/steep drops to the side of the path in places - take care in windy weather. The many sections through woodland are boggy or muddy underfoot, especially after wet weather.

Take care walking along the escarpment of the Hambleton Hills - sheer cliffs in places. There are a number of ascents and descents along this walk, especially through the many side-valleys of Ryedale.

The woodland and valley paths are muddy underfoot. Take care walking along the roads through Cold Kirby and Rievaulx.

Ascents:	Hambleton Street:	332 metres

Viewpoints:
The climb along the old Kepwick Road from Arden Hall to Dale Town common offers wonderful views of Thorodale, Ryedale and the Tabular Hills through the trees.
The extensive views from Boltby Scar across the Vale of York towards the Pennines are the highlight of this walk.
Rievaulx Abbey provides a fitting climax to the walk.

FACILITIES
. . . .

Hawnby	Inn / B&B / Shop / Café / Phone
Cold Kirby	B&B
Scawton	Inn / B&B / Phone
Rievaulx	Shop / Café / Bus / Phone / Toilets / Info
Helmsley	Inn / B&B / Shop / P.O. / Café / Bus / Phone / Toilets / Info / YH

ROUTE DESCRIPTION
. . . .

(Map Seventeen)

From the T-junction at the top of Hawnby village, turn left along the road (SP 'Kepwick') passing the pub on your left and follow the road out of the village then straight on down *(ignore turnings off)* for 0.5 miles to reach Church Bridge across the River Rye (SE 535 899). Immediately after the bridge take the track to the left through a gate (SP 'Arden Hall'), after which head straight on with the river on your left for a short distance then, where the river bends away to the left, head up to the right along a grassy path towards a telegraph pole. As you reach the telegraph pole the path becomes clearer and leads straight on through a gate along a tree-shaded track up to reach a second gate, immediately after which turn right and head up the bank then, just before the next gate in the top corner of the field, head round to the left along a level track across the top of the field to reach a gate that leads into woodland (SE 530 899). Head through the gate and walk straight on through the woods (Nag's Head Wood) for 0.25 miles to reach a fork in the track, where you bear right and follow the clear track for a further 0.3 miles to eventually reach a gate at the end of the woods. After this gate, bear left down the grassy bank to reach a track along the bottom of the valley. Turn right along this track for a short distance then, just before the gate across the track that leads into woodland, head right (off the track) across the field *(same field you have just walked down from Nag's Head Wood)* alongside the fence/woodland on your left (wooded ravine of Stoney Gill Hole down to your left) to soon reach a gate in the field corner (SE 522 903). Head through the gate and follow the track down through woodland to join the road where you turn left along the road to reach a junction of lanes at the entrance to Arden Hall (SE 519 905).

At this junction, carry straight on up along the unsurfaced road towards 'Kepwick' ('Unsuitable for Motors') and follow this climbing quite steeply up through woodland. After about 0.3 miles the track levels out for a while and leads through a gate across the track just after which the track climbs up again passing some old quarry workings on your left, 100 yards after which you reach a fork in the track. Turn left at this fork (back on yourself slightly) along a stony track (waymarker) and follow this up onto flat grassy moorland. The stony track soon disappears; however, carry straight on along the indistinct grassy track that soon leads down to reach a gate in a wall at the bottom of a shallow dip (head of Stoney Gill Hole - SE 511 902). Head through the gate and follow the track up to soon join a wall on your left. However, as soon as you join the wall (by the gate in this wall) bear very gradually to the right (away from the track and wall) across the open, grassy moorland *(heading in a SSW direction)*. At first the path is unclear, however, after approx. 250 yards you join a more defined path (just where the wall across to your left bends away to the left) that gently meanders across the middle of the moorland of Dale Town Common (heading in a SW direction) for 0.75 miles to reach a gate in the far corner of the enclosed moorland that leads onto the wide, walled track of Hambleton Street (SE 504 890).

Head straight across along the farm lane opposite (SP 'Cleveland Way') that leads to High Paradise Farm. Follow the track passing to the right of the farm buildings and then straight on down through the farm gates (track becomes a metalled road), after which follow the road gently curving round to the left into Boltby Forest. Continue straight on along this road gently dropping down for 0.25 miles then, where it bends sharply down to the right, carry straight on through a gate (SP 'Cleveland Way'). After the gate, follow the level grassy track straight on across the field to reach a gate that leads into woodland where you carry straight on along the track rising gently up through the woods to join the road at Sneck Yate (SE 507 875). At the road take the track opposite that leads up to a gate (SP 'Cleveland Way, Sutton Bank'), after which a very clear path heads straight on gently climbing along the top of the escarpment for 0.5 miles to reach the conspicuous landmark of High Barn, sheltered by a copse of trees. *Caution: there are cliffs to the side of the path between High Barn and Whitestone Cliff.* From High Barn, continue straight on along the clear path that follows the top of the escarpment for 0.75 miles passing above the cliffs of Boltby Scar up to reach the slight promontory of Boltby Scar hill-fort, with its scattering of trees *(just beyond which are the remains of the prehistoric hill-fort)*. From this promontory, carry straight on for a further 1.25 miles following the edge of the escarpment as it very gradually sweeps round to the right towards the next promontory of Whitestone Cliff (SE 506 839). As you reach this promontory (where the path turns sharp left to run along the top of Whitestone Cliff) take the BW to the left through a small gate (SP 'Dialstone Farm'). Head straight on alongside the stone wall on your right for a short distance then follow the perimeter of the field as it bends round to the left then head straight on keeping to the wall/field-edge for 0.75 miles *(path switches to the other side of the wall after 0.5 miles)* all the way to reach a road beside the entrance to Dialstone Farm (large radio mast). At the farm, turn right along the road to quickly reach a T-junction where you turn left along the road for 0.75 miles into Cold Kirby (SE 533 845).

(Map Eighteen)

Follow the road into Cold Kirby ('Dead End' sign) then, where the road forks as you reach the small tree-shaded green, follow the right-hand road passing the church on your left (SP) then continue along this road out of the village (road becomes a track). Carry straight on along this track then, where it forks after 150 yards (clearer track bends sharp left), follow the right-hand track straight on through a gate. Follow this rough track straight on across fields then, where it bends away to the left, continue straight on along the right-hand side of a hedge (SP) across a field down to reach the top of the steep wooded slopes of Flassen Dale (SE 537 838). Enter the woods and bear down to the right to quickly join a clear track which almost immediately forks - follow the left-hand track then immediately head to the left off this track along a narrow path that slants steeply down to reach a track along the valley bottom. Turn left along this track then almost immediately turn right up along a clear path that leads steeply up through woodland to a stile at the top of the hill. Cross the stile and head straight across the field and over a stile just beyond a farm track. Cross this stile and continue straight on across three fields alongside the fence/hedge on your right to reach a gate in the field corner near the top of the wooded valley of Brignal Gill (SE 545 834). Cross the stile to the right beside this gate then, keeping close to the fence/wooded valley on your left, follow the grassy track swinging sharply round to the left around the head of the wooded valley *(do not follow the grassy track up through the valley)* round to reach a reach a stile over a fence. Cross this stile then bear to the right across the middle of the next field to reach the left-hand of two gates in the far top corner of the field just by the farm buildings *(do not enter the farmyard)*. After the gate, head straight on across the next field alongside the fence/farm buildings on your right to reach another gate in the field corner (waymarker), after which turn right across the next field and through a kissing gate that lead onto an enclosed path that brings you out in the centre of Scawton *(Hare Inn short detour to the right along the road)*.

Head left along the road out of the village and follow the road down for 0.5 miles then, where the road bends sharply to the right (road 'chevron' sign), head straight on through a gate along a farm track towards 'Stocking House Farm'; however, immediately after the gate forsake the farm track for a path that branches off to the left down into Spring Wood (SP 'Nettle Dale'). Follow the clear path down through the woods to reach a crossroads of paths and tracks (Bridge Road) at the bottom of the valley of Nettle Dale in a clearing (SE 556 846). Walk across the track (SP 'Cleveland Way'), over stepping stones across a stream and up through a bridlegate, just after which you join a rough track (with the clearer track just to your left) where you turn right then almost immediately left over a FB across a stream. After the FB, head to the right across the field to quickly join a rutted track which you follow straight on across the left-hand side of the field *(heading towards the small lake)* to reach a gate across the track just before the lake. Head through the gate and follow the clear track straight on through woodland to soon emerge out into a clearing (with the lake to your right), where you follow the clear track swinging round to the left heading up through a grassy side-valley following a line of telegraph poles. Continue up along the track heading up through this wooded side-valley (following the telegraph poles), with the woodland of Spring Wood and valley slopes gradually closing in, for 0.25 miles all the way to emerge from the trees to reach a wall across your path at the top of this wooded side-valley (SE 556 851). *

The legal line of the Right of Way up through this wooded side-valley differs slightly from the ground. Three-quarters of the way up this side-valley, the BW braches off to the left slightly up and then across the wooded valley slope (with the track just down to your right) to emerge from the trees where you reach a wall across your path at the top of this wooded side-valley. At the time of writing, this slight deviation from the track was difficult to follow and unclear on the ground.

As you reach the wall at the top of this wooded side-valley (with the wall in front of you), turn right (alongside the wall on your left) to quickly reach a gate, after which head straight on across the field alongside the wall on your left to reach another gate in the field corner, after which carry straight on alongside the fence on your left then, half way across this field, turn left through a gate in a fence (by a small section of stone wall). After the gate, head straight up across the field to reach a gate between the two large barns that leads into the farmyard of Reins Farm (waymarker). Head through the gate and follow the track round to the right through the farmyard then, as you reach the back of the farmhouse, follow the track down to your left into woodland (SP). Follow this farm track slanting quite steeply down through the woods to the floor of Low Gill where you follow the track over a small stream then up and round to the right to reach a road (SE 566 855).

Turn left up along the road for 150 yards then take the first turning on the right towards 'Tylas Farm' and 'Barnclose Farm'. Follow this lane down through woodland then, where it levels out, you reach a junction of tracks - turn right back on yourself slightly along a stony track that leads down for 0.25 miles to reach Bow Bridge over the River Rye. Cross the bridge and carry straight on along the track for about 150 yards then take the FP to the right through a bridlegate in a fence (SP 'Rievaulx'). After the bridlegate, head left across the field (river to your right) to soon reach a bridlegate in a line of trees beside the River Rye on your right, after which turn left alongside the fence and overgrown banks of the old canal on your left across fields *(heading towards Rievaulx Abbey in the distance)* then, as you reach the houses on the edge Rievaulx village, carry straight on along the grassy track through a gate (and over a small stream) then pass to the right-hand side of a low stone barn (stables) through more gates to join the road at Rievaulx village (SE 575 851).

(Map Nineteen)

Turn right along the road passing Rievaulx Abbey on your left and follow the road for a further 0.5 miles to a T-junction beside Rievaulx

Bridge. Turn left here (SP 'Helmsley') and follow the road straight on for 0.3 miles then follow the road as it bends round and up to the left *(use roadside path)* for a short distance then take the track to the right (SP 'Cleveland Way, Helmsley 2 miles') up into woodland (SE 580 841). Follow this clear, wide path climbing steadily up through Quarry Bank Wood for almost 0.5 miles to reach a crossroads of tracks, where you carry straight on to quickly emerge from the woods at the top of Whinny Bank. Carry straight on along the clear, wide (level) path along the top of Whinny Bank, with fields to your left and the steep wooded slopes of Whinny Bank to your right, for a further 0.5 miles to reach a clear farm track just beyond Griff Lodge (SE 590 834).

Head straight across the track (SP) along the path ahead that quickly joins an old wall on your left - follow this path straight on through trees/undergrowth along the edge of the woodland (with the old wall on your left) for 0.25 miles to reach a bridlegate across your path that leads into woodland. Head through the bridlegate and follow the path steeply down into and up out of the small wooded ravine of Blackdale Howl (steps) and out of the woods (SE 595 836). As you emerge from the woods at the top of the steps, turn right and follow the clear path along the perimeter of the field (fields to your left and woodland to your right) for almost 0.5 miles *(Helmsley castle in the distance)* then follow the enclosed path bending sharp left then sharp right (very obvious 'dog-leg' in the path), after which the path becomes a track, which gradually becomes clearer *(still heading towards Helmsley Castle)* and then becomes a lane that lead back into Helmsley.

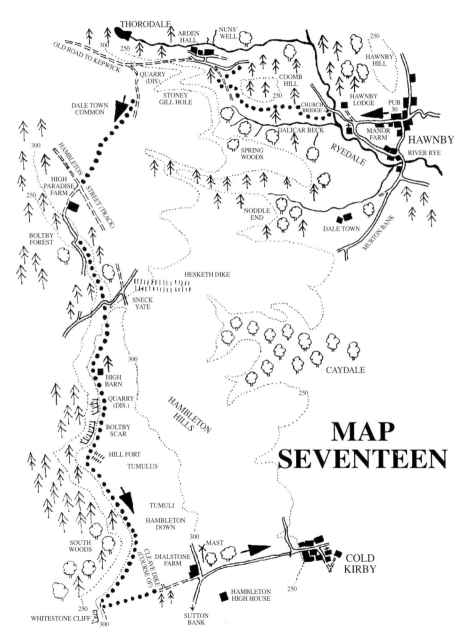

THORODALE

OLD ROAD TO KEPWICK

300
250

ARDEN HALL

NUNS' WELL

250

HAWNBY HILL

QUARRY (DIS)

COOMB HILL

250

HAWNBY LODGE

PUB 30

DALE TOWN COMMON

STONEY GILL HOLE

CHURCH BRIDGE

MANOR FARM

HAWNBY

300

HAMBLETON STREET (TRACK)

DALICAR BECK

RYEDALE

RIVER RYE

HIGH PARADISE FARM

250

SPRING WOODS

BOLTBY FOREST

NODDLE END

DALE TOWN

MURTON BANK

HESKETH DIKE

SNECK YATE

300

HIGH BARN

QUARRY (DIS.)

HAMBLETON HILLS

250

CAYDALE

BOLTBY SCAR

HILL FORT

TUMULUS

MAP
SEVENTEEN

TUMULI

HAMBLETON DOWN

300

MAST

SOUTH WOODS

CLEAVE DIKE (COURSE OF)

DIALSTONE FARM

COLD KIRBY

HAMBLETON HIGH HOUSE

250

250

WHITESTONE CLIFF

300

SUTTON BANK

189

MAP EIGHTEEN

MAP NINETEEN

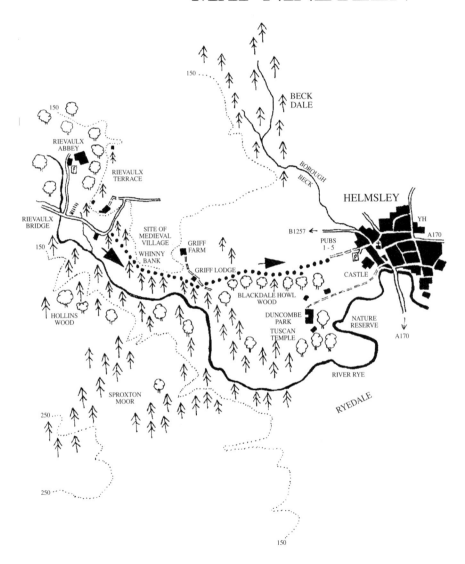

150

BECK
DALE

BOROUGH
BECK

HELMSLEY

YH

B1257 ←

A170

RIEVAULX
ABBEY

150

RIEVAULX
TERRACE

RIEVAULX
BRIDGE

150

SITE OF
MEDIEVAL
VILLAGE

GRIFF
FARM

WHINNY
BANK

GRIFF LODGE

PUBS
1 - 5

CASTLE

BLACKDALE HOWL
WOOD

HOLLINS
WOOD

DUNCOMBE
PARK

NATURE
RESERVE

A170

TUSCAN
TEMPLE

SPROXTON
MOOR

RIVER RYE

RYEDALE

250

250

150

RYEDALE, or Rye Dale according to the Ordnance Survey, is arguably the finest valley in the North York Moors. The River Rye rises on the flanks of Whorlton Moor high amongst the desolate Cleveland Hills some six miles north-west of Hawnby, cradled by Osmotherley Moor to the west and Snilesworth Moor to the east. But this desolation is short lived as the infant Rye quickly leaves the high moorland with its underlying sandstones to make a leisurely journey through the Hambleton and Tabular Hills whose alkaline limestone and calcareous sandstone rocks support fertile soils; within two miles of taking its first watery cascade Ryedale has matured into a valley of unparalleled beauty.

Ryedale is characterised by three things. Firstly its trees, as this steep-sided valley is cloaked in primeval oak woodland. These oak woods once covered much of the North York Moors before man began to clear the forests for agriculture. Fortunately the steep slopes have prevented total clearance and these trees now stand as some of the last surviving examples of native woodland in the country. Secondly, its side-valleys - and there are a lot of them - Eskerdale, Thorodale, Gowerdale, Caydale, Flassen Dale, Nettle Dale...the list is endless. *"Caydale is a little dream-world flanked by woods, with the great mass of Easterside Hill beyond. In spring and summer it is a paradise of wild flowers. Pure Ryedale country this, which I tremble to write about lest it be spoilt!"* **(A. J. Brown 'Fair North Riding' 1952)**. These sylvan valleys are characterised by very steep sides, the result of erosion from countless springs that bubble up from the underlying rock. Thirdly, its villages. Here you will find villages as pretty as any in the Cotswolds but surrounded by far superior scenery with picture-postcard houses of soft honey-coloured stone set beneath red pantiles clinging to the steep valley sides. Ryedale's largest tributary, Bilsdale, swells the waters of the River Rye before flowing past the romantic ruins of Rievaulx Abbey and on to Helmsley. From Helmsley Ryedale's character changes as the river flows out across the flat and fertile Vale of Pickering with its patchwork of fields, quiet lanes bordered by rich hedgerows and picturesque villages before flowing into the River Derwent near Malton. The name of this valley has also been adopted by Ryedale District Council which, at 575 square miles, stands as one of the largest district authorities in the country whose boundaries stretch far beyond the valley of the Rye.

Arden Hall

ARDEN HALL has a romantic setting in the deep wooded valley of Thorodale. This beautiful and exquisitely proportioned three-storey building dates from the 17th Century, although the building stands on the site of a 12th Century Benedictine nunnery, fragments of which remain inside the Hall including a medieval fireplace. The wonderful gardens of Arden Hall are dominated by a billowing yew hedge that is said to have been planted by the nuns of Arden who came to this secluded spot in 1150 until their lands and nunnery were taken from them following the Dissolution of the Monasteries Act for the Suppression of the Lesser Monasteries in 1536. It was never a prosperous nunnery with limited lands farmed directly from Arden, unlike neighbouring Rievaulx Abbey whose extensive lands were controlled through a system of granges (monastic farms). After the Dissolution of the Monasteries the nunnery's lands came into the ownership of Ralfe Tankarde, whose family later changed their name to Tancred, and the Hall remained in their ownership until 1897 when it was bought by the 6th Earl of Mexborough. Mary, Queen of Scots reputedly stayed at Arden during the mid 16th Century. The Hall is still occupied by the Earls of Mexborough whose 13,000-acre estate, including much of Hawnby village, provides valuable grouse shooting moors. Hidden in trees behind the Hall are a series of crystal-clear springs, with one particular man-made pool still known as Nuns' Well. From Arden an old road heads up alongside Thorodale before crossing the old drovers' road of Hambleton Street and then steeply down to Kepwick. Images of stagecoaches rattling up this old lane and trains of packhorses spring to mind for this is one of many old roads throughout the North York Moors that have never been improved. From this road there are wonderful views across the deep, wooded valley of Thorodale with its glittering lake and heather moorland stretching hazily into the distance.

HAMBLETON DROVE ROAD, otherwise known as Hambleton Street, was once an important drovers' road between Scotland and the market towns of York, Malton and the South of England. This route was primarily used as a drovers' road from the 17th Century until the early 19th Century when great herds of livestock, in particular cattle, were a common sight as they were being taken on hoof to satisfy the growing appetites of the burgeoning southern urban markets. The expanding railway network during the 1840s heralded the terminal decline of these drovers' roads, although they continued to be used up until the end of the 19th Century. What a sight it must have been with mile upon mile of cattle, pigs, geese, sheep and turkeys on their way to market - this was once one of the busiest roads in Britain made busier by the fact that the drovers used it to avoid paying the tolls of the lowland turnpike roads. *"...the road was the main cattle-way to and from the Border; and many a tale could be told of the feuds and fights among the old drovers."* **(A. J. Brown 1952)**. Stories are told of how the drovers, upon reaching their destination, used to send their dogs back to find their own way home. These clever dogs apparently called at the many inns along the route for refreshment and shelter and the innkeepers would charge the drover on his next visit! There were four drovers' inns along this stretch across the Hambleton Hills with the Chequers above Osmotherley now a farmhouse, ruinous Limekiln House stood along the flat grassy section above Kepwick, Dialstone is now a farmhouse whilst the Hambleton Inn near Sutton Bank is still a pub.

This road is one of the oldest in the country dating back much further than the days of the drovers to prehistoric times as such high-level routes avoided the more dangerous valley roads. Unbelievably one thousand years ago this was classed as the main road between York and Yarm where it crossed the River Tees and continued northwards towards the border with Scotland. The road was used by the Roman legions, it is said that William the Conqueror came this way after his Harrying of the North in 1069 and in 1322 King Edward II and his army were pursued by Robert Bruce along this road after a fruitless campaign in Scotland only to be beaten by the Scots at the Battle of Byland above Oldstead on the south-western edge of the Hambleton Hills. Today most of the route has been incorporated into our present road system; however, the section across the Hambleton Hills from Scarth Nick near Osmotherley to Oldstead can be easily traced and remains as a grassy track for most of the way. Undeniably one of the finest walks in England, you too can follow in the footsteps of Bronze Age people, Romans, Kings of England, monks and drovers.

THE HAMBLETON HILLS rise dramatically from the vales of York and Mowbray to 400 metres above sea level on the summit of the looming bulk of Black Hambleton, which marks the northern limit of the Hambleton Hills. From Black Hambleton the escarpment continues as the Cleveland Hills, sweeping north-eastwards towards Teesside. These two ranges of hills combine to form a continuous escarpment that sweeps for over 40 miles from Ampleforth in the south to Guisborough in the north. It is these hills, along with the coast to the east and the Tabular Hills to the south, that make the North York Moors such a distinct area; no other National Park has such well-defined natural boundaries. This escarpment was formed during the latter stages of the last Ice Age when ice-flows from the

Cumbrian mountains flowed eastwards across the Pennines. Blocked by the Scandinavian glaciers in what is now the North Sea, the ice turned to flow down the Vale of York. As these glaciers began to melt, great torrents of water carved channels between the ice and the land; it was these meltwaters that formed the sheer escarpment of the Hambleton Hills. The Hambleton Hills are made up of limestones and calcareous grits from the late Jurassic period over 150 million years ago, which provide well-drained fertile soils. It is, however, still quite a surprise to see crops such as wheat growing right up to the escarpment edge - I just hope that the farmers have had their tractors' brakes properly tested! Above all, this escarpment provides some of the finest views in England with the Pennines forming a backdrop to a far-reaching vista of farmland; it is said that you can watch a train leave York station and follow it all the way to Darlington, although why you would want to do that, I do not know! Alf Wight, known to millions as James Herriot, declared it to be the finest view in England and this was also where the young William Wordsworth and his new wife Mary Hutchinson watched the sunset on their wedding night. *"Every day is different up here and often the far hills are dreamlike with distance, but there are other times, on the frosty mornings or after a night's wind, when you can almost reach out and touch the flat top of Penhill, when you can look down Wensleydale and peep into the entrance of Coverdale with the long summit of Great Whernside rearing above its neighbours. On those days the mighty plain seems like a narrow valley between the two ranges of hills."* (**J. Herriot 'James Herriot's Yorkshire' 1979**).

For me, the finest stretch of this escarpment runs from Sneck Yate to Whitestone Cliff. A vast three-dimensional map of Yorkshire unfolds beneath your feet as you follow the gently curving cliff-edge along Boltby Scar. On a fine day flat-topped Penhill is clearly visible above the broad acres of Wensleydale whilst just to the left of it stands Great Whernside some 30 miles away. Immediately below are several small villages reposing amongst the small wooded foothills with Boltby village, its large forest and small reservoir clearly identifiable. Not surprisingly, this elevated escarpment is rich in Bronze and Iron

Age remains, particularly earthworks and dykes. The extensive Cleave Dyke system runs from beyond Sutton Bank to Arden Great Moor and was built originally to define the boundary between tribes. Unfortunately, much of this earthwork system has been lost under the plough over the centuries; however, good sections remain at Sutton Bank and Hesketh Dike. Towards the end of the Bronze Age as population levels grew, so did the need for more defensive sites. A hill fort was built on the promontory of Boltby Scar about 4,000 years ago, its earth ditches and banks surviving four millennia until they were unceremoniously ploughed out by a farmer 40 years ago. Thankfully a small section of rampart remains near to the cliff-edge. The Bronze Age and Iron Age peoples were generally peaceful farmers as the thousands of prehistoric tumuli, dykes, field systems and other remains testify - there are only a handful of defensive hill-forts within the North York Moors. As the escarpment turns sharply left towards Whitestone Cliff a small promontory juts out to give a superb view of the cliffs as well as Gormire Lake sheltered amongst trees. This lake was formed during the last Ice Age when a landslide blocked a meltwater channel and is unique as it has no streams feeding or leaving it, underground drainage regulates the flow. As you may expect, many legends surround it. Local people once believed it to be bottomless, whilst another tale tells of a submerged village, including a church complete with spire! The Devil, dressed as the Abbot of Rievaulx, is also said to have lured a knight on horseback to his death over the crags at a spot still known as White Mare Crag, the other name for Whitestone Cliff.

DIALSTONE FARM was once an inn on the ancient drover's road known as Hambleton Street, which passed its front door, although it is now a working farm. The name Dialstone refers to the weighing machine used by jockeys, as the surrounding flat plateau, known as Hambleton Down, was once a major racecourse whose firm yet soft turf is still considered to be amongst the best in the country for racehorse training. The Hambleton Races began in the early 17th Century and soon developed a great following with cups given and presented by George I and Queen Anne, culminating in such prestigious races as Her Majesty's Gold Cup during the 18th Century when the racecourse eclipsed that of York and Newmarket. The isolated location meant that other racecourses with better amenities, not to mention being less exposed to the elements, gradually won favour. Racehorses are still trained in the area with several large stables nearby.

COLD KIRBY has a rather exposed location on the gently sloping Hambeleton Hills; those early settlers who named their village appear to have had a rather dry sense of humour as it literally means a 'cold hamlet by the church'. This attractive linear village has changed little since medieval times with cottages and farms lining the single street and narrow strip-fields, or crofts, running back from the village; many of the houses were rebuilt in stone during the 17th and 18th centuries. St Michael's Church dates from the 12th Century, although almost completely rebuilt in 1841; all that remains of the original church is the font and a 13th Century bell. Unbelievably, this remote parish church was originally ministered by the Order of Knights Templars. This secretive yet powerful military religious order was established in 1120 to protect pilgrims and knights during the Holy Land Crusades and soon accrued great wealth and lands which they used to finance their campaigns. The Order was suppressed in 1314 on the orders of the Pope because they had become too powerful and threatened the authority of Rome. After this suppression, St Michael's passed into the ownership of the Knights Hospitallers, a similar but less powerful Order, who held it until the Reformation. A story is told of a monk from Byland Abbey who served as the church priest and had a secret fancy-woman in the village. When he died he came back to haunt the village and, so frightened were the villagers, that they exhumed his body and threw it into the 'bottomless' Gormire Lake.

SCAWTON lies on a shelf of land above Bradley Howl, indeed Scawton means 'farm in a hollow' in Old Norse. Howl, incidentally, is the local term for the small, deep valleys that can be found throughout the Tabular Hills. This quiet village is off the beaten track away from the tourist crowds, but this has not always been the case as the road through the village used to be a main road in medieval times known as Sperragate that connected Helmsley with the busy road of Hambleton Street via Rievaulx. It was developed by the monks to provide a quick route between Byland and Rievaulx abbeys as well as to their granges and the important trade routes. It is said that the Hare Inn was built by the monks of either Rievaulx or Byland in the early 12th Century to refresh travellers on this ancient road, although there is little evidence to support this. There has definitely been an inn on this site since the early 17th Century when the farmer supplemented his income by brewing ale, although the present building is 18th Century. The pub retains a great deal of character with open fires, low ceilings, interesting bric-a-brac and lots of nooks and crannies.

Scawton's unique Norman church, dedicated to St Mary, has altered little since it was built by the monks of Byland Abbey in 1146, its age apparent from its irregular windows, bowing walls and characteristic zig-zag pattern in the stonework around the door; note the sad memorial to the five crew members of a Halifax bomber that crashed nearby in 1945. *"At the present time this ancient fabric is in such an interesting state of decay, that it is not considered safe to toll the bell!"* **(G. Frank 'Ryedale and North Yorkshire Antiquities' 1888).** In 1138 a group of Cistercian monks travelled from Cumbria to North Yorkshire in the hope of establishing a new monastery. They settled near Old Byland at what is now Tylas Farm and built a grange at Old Byland and also re-built the former Saxon church there. However, they could hear the bells of Rievaulx a few miles down the valley so after four years they moved to Oldstead and then finally settled at Byland Abbey near Ampleforth in 1177 where they built their magnificent church. It was whilst they were at Old Byland that they built this small church at Scawton. The church is noted for its 'piscina', a stone basin used to wash the holy vessels, and two 'sedilias' or priest's seats cut into the wall. It is thought that the font, altar stone and one of the bells may have been brought to the church from Old Byland making the bell one of the oldest in the country. *"The base of an old cross is by the village pond, and standing neighbourly with the grey* *cottages is a small church whose rough walls are weathered by the storms of nearly 800 winters."* (**A. Mee 'Yorkshire North Riding' 1941**). The square stone base of Scawton Cross, whose shaft has long since disappeared, can now be found situated against the wall of the churchyard near to a bench; the village pond was filled in many years ago. This cross may well have been erected in the village by the monks who built the church, it may even be a much older preaching cross.

NETTLE DALE is one of Ryedale's largest and most attractive tributaries with the hidden valleys of Low Gill, Tanker Dale, Flassen Dale and Bradley Howl converging near a delightful trio of small lakes to form Nettle Dale, aptly named indeed as you will find out if you venture through the undergrowth in shorts! Nettle Dale is a haven of peace and quiet as only footpaths and bridleways venture into this unfrequented valley. *"Sharp and sudden these huge slopes sweep down into narrow valleys; for this, the eastward corner of the Hambleton Hills, is an intricate network of deep hollows, fringed with woods and musical with running streams. And down each one of these winding vales there sings the fresh wind of the moors, keen and stimulating, carrying the scents of gorse and heather into the denser air of the low bottoms, so that each one of them is bright and breezy, and the thick shadows flung across the streamlets by the woods are continually shaken."* (**A. Norway 'Highways and Byways in Yorkshire' 1899**). Cloaked in old oak woodland with crystal-clear streams gushing from numerous springs, the area is also home to a diverse range of wildlife including the poisonous adder.

RIEVAULX, pronounced 'Reevo', is a small village of pale stone cottages set beneath red pantiles or the occasional thatch, dotted along the narrow road that climbs out of the confines of Ryedale. A picturesque scene indeed, but one often overlooked by visitors for it is completely overshadowed by the awe-inspiring ruins of Rievaulx Abbey. If your first sight of this colossal masterpiece in stone is on this walk then pause at Bow Bridge, free your mind of clutter and walk along the Old Canal towards the ruins of the finest Cistercian Abbey in the British Isles; you will not be disappointed. *"...set like a jewel in this romantic glen enfolded by heights of noble trees rising to the moors."* (**A. Mee 1941**).

In 1132 twelve monks came over from Clairvaux in France to establish the first Cistercian abbey in the North and what would become the 'mother' church of the Cistercian Order in England. They had been given about 1,000 acres of wilderness, wasteland and scrub by Walter Espec of Helmsley Castle, which met their requirements exactly as theirs was an Order of poverty and simplicity. These French monks named their abbey after the valley in which it was situated - Rievaulx means the 'valley of the Rye' in Norman French. Their land holdings, albeit poor moorland, soon began to increase as Norman lords sought favour with the monks and, they hoped, a passage into heaven. It was during the rule of St Aelred (1147 - 1167), Rievaulx's third Abbot, that the abbey prospered and when most of the major building work took place. St Aelred was, by all accounts, a man of great character, skill and power, a man whose influence was still felt four centuries later at the time of its suppression. He developed the abbey into the largest monastic establishment in England, which at its height had 140 choir monks and over 500 lay brothers. It was these lay brothers who were at the heart of the success of the Cistercian Order as they could work the land on behalf of the monks whilst still observing some monastic orders so overcoming the problem of the Order's strict rules and regime of prayer. By the early 13th Century Rievaulx Abbey had acquired several thousand acres of land predominantly in Bilsdale, Ryedale and Bransdale but also in Wensleydale, Swaledale, Airedale and Teesside on which they developed sheep farming controlled through a system of granges. Although wool was the main source of their wealth, the monks also developed ironstone mining, horse breeding, brewing, milling and fishing; they were entrepreneurs way ahead of their time who changed the way farming was carried out in this country. Unfortunately the fortunes of the abbey turned for the worse during the 13th Century due to poor wool prices as well as debts accrued due to land purchases and construction work. This was compounded in the 14th Century when conflicts across the border spilled south and Scottish raids became more frequent, in particular following the nearby Battle of Byland in 1322 when Edward II's army was beaten and many granges were attacked. The system of granges was abandoned and farming was either carried out directly from the abbey or the farms were let to tenants. When the abbey was suppressed in 1538 on the orders of Henry VIII there were only twenty-two monks left.

Following its suppression, the abbey buildings as well as its lands in Bilsdale and Ryedale were sold, at a knocked down price, to the Earl of Rutland from nearby Helmsley Castle, the ownership of which eventually came to Sir Charles Duncombe whose descendant, the Earl of Feversham, still owns the ruins, although they are now managed by English Heritage. These romantic ruins, cradled by the steep yet soft slopes of Ryedale, are dominated by the towering Transepts of the original 12th Century church as well as the graceful arches and columns of the early 13th Century Choir and Presbytery, built to hold the shrine of St Aelred. With the exception of the Presbytery, almost the entire abbey was built within sixty years during the 12th Century. Note that the church has more of a south to north alignment rather than the traditional east to west, a result of the narrow confines of the valley. Historians also believe that the monks tried to create more space along the valley floor by diverting the course of the River Rye, and then utilising the course of the original river as a canal on which stone could be transported for the building of the abbey as well as ironstone for smelting; some historians dispute this and claim that the canals are man-made. Either way, this is probably the earliest industrial canal system in this country. The Church of St Mary in the village of Rievaulx was built in 1906 on the site of the former Gate-Chapel of the abbey and incorporates a great deal of stonework from the original 13th Century structure. The historic Rievaulx Bridge was built in the 13th Century by the monks but was unfortunately severely damaged by floods in 1754. Bow Bridge was built in the 18th Century to the design of the famous Georgian designer John Carr.

To the east of the abbey on the bank above the valley are the famous 18th Century gardens of Rievaulx Terrace. This beautiful landscaped garden of lawns and trees boasts a temple at each end of the terrace in the Ionic and Tuscan style. Rievaulx Terrace was developed in 1758 as part of the Duncombe Park estate to provide a formal garden where wealthy people could stroll and picnic as well as admire the carefully planned views through gaps in the trees down towards the ruins of the abbey and beyond to the wild moors; Turner and Wordsworth gained inspiration from this elevated garden for paint and poem alike. *"All the beauty and charm of this lovely district is accentuated in Ryedale, and when we have accomplished the three long uphill miles to Rievaulx, and come out upon the broad grassy terrace above the abbey, we seem to have entered a Land of Beulah."* **(G. Home 'Yorkshire' 1908)**.

DUNCOMBE PARK comprises an imposing house and extensive landscaped gardens to the west of Helmsley. From Rievaulx Bridge, the final section of *The Inn Way... to the North York Moors* climbs the wooded slopes of Whinny Bank, route of an intended carriage link between Rievaulx Terrace and Duncombe Park, to reach Griff Lodge near to which stands Griff Farm, one-time grange of Rievaulx Abbey and the site of a 'lost' medieval village. The path continues through the ancient Blackdale Howl Wood and skirts Duncombe Park with glimpses of Ryedale and the house of Duncombe Park through the trees. Sir Charles Duncombe, a wealthy London banker and Lord Mayor of London, bought Helmsley Castle and its estate in 1689 on the death of the Duke of Buckingham. His nephew Thomas Browne, who later adopted the Duncombe name, inherited the estate and built Duncombe Park in 1713 as the family home instead of the rather cold and damp castle. The house was designed by local architect William Wakefield with, so it is said, a little help from Sir John Vanbrugh. The wings were added in 1845 and were designed by Sir Charles Barry, more famous as the architect of the Houses of Parliament. In 1879 the original 18th Century house was all but destroyed by fire, although the façade was saved, and was sympathetically restored and rebuilt. The house is still occupied by Lord Feversham, descendant of the Duncombe family, and is open to the public. The vast formal landscaped gardens are of particular note, a superb example of bold yet romantic 18th Century planned gardens with terraces, temples, sweeping parkland and mature woodland designed to complement the natural landscape. Over 200 acres of gardens and parkland are now protected as a National Nature Reserve.

BIBLIOGRAPHY

The following books are listed as follows: author, title, date first published and publisher.

W. Andrews, 'Historic Yorkshire', 1883, Reeves and Turner.

G. Frank, 'Ryedale and North Yorkshire Antiquities', 1888, Elliot Stock.

W. Andrews, 'Yorkshire in Olden Times', 1890, A. Brown & Sons Ltd.

Rev. J. C. Atkinson, 'Forty Years in a Moorland Parish', 1891, Macmillan & Co.

W. Andrews, 'Bygone Yorkshire', 1892, A. Brown & Sons Ltd.

A. H. Norway, 'Highways and Byways in Yorkshire', 1899, Macmillan and Co. Ltd.

J. S. Fletcher, 'The Enchanting North', 1908, Eveleigh Nash.

G. Home, 'Yorkshire', 1908, A. & C. Black Ltd.

A. P. Wilson, 'Yorkshire Moors and Dales', circa 1910, A. Brown & Sons Ltd.

W. Edwards, 'The Early History of the North Riding', 1924, A. Brown & Sons Ltd.

F. R. Pearson, 'Yorkshire', 1928, Alfred Knopf Ltd.

A. H. Smith, 'The Place-Names of the North Riding of Yorkshire', 1928, Cambridge University Press.

E. Pontefract and M. Hartley, 'Yorkshire Tour', 1939, J. M. Dent & Sons Ltd.

A. Mee, 'Yorkshire North Riding', 1941, Hodder and Stoughton Ltd. (Copyright © Arthur Mee 1941)

A. J. Brown, 'Broad Acres', 1948, Country Life.

C. E. M. Joad (Editor), 'The English Counties', circa 1949, Odhams Press.

G. B. Wood, 'Yorkshire Tribute', 1950, Methuen & Co. Ltd.

A. J. Brown, 'Fair North Riding', 1952, Country Life.

J. and R. Fairfax-Blakeborough, ' The Spirit of Yorkshire', 1954, B. T. Batsford Ltd.

M. Hartley and J. Ingilby, 'The Wonders of Yorkshire', 1959, J. M. Dent & Sons Ltd.

H. J. Scott, 'Portrait of Yorkshire', 1965, Robert Hale.

N. Pevsner, 'Yorkshire The North Riding', 1966, Penguin Books.

J. Hadfield (Editor), 'The Shell Guide to England', 1970, Michael Joseph.

R. H. Hayes, 'A History of Rosedale', 1971, North York Moors National Park

R. J. W. Hammond (Editor), 'Complete Yorkshire', 1973, Ward Lock.

A. Wainwright, 'A Coast to Coast Walk', 1973, Westmorland Gazette (Michael Joseph Ltd., current publishers 1987). Approx. 75 words Copyright © the Estate of the Late A. Wainwright 1987.

R. H. Hayes and J. G. Rutter, 'Rosedale Mines and Railway', 1974, Scarborough Archaeological and Historical Society.

R. Carter, 'Yorkshire Churches', 1976, Watmoughs Ltd.

H. Mead, 'Inside the North York Moors', 1978, David & Charles.

J. Herriot, 'James Herriot's Yorkshire', 1979, Michael Joseph.

M. Colbeck, 'Yorkshire Moorlands', 1983, B. T. Batsford Ltd.

M. Parker, 'The North York Moors and Coast', 1984, Discovery Guides.

Nicholas Rhea, 'Portrait of the North York Moors', 1985, Robert Hale.

AA / Ordnance Survey Leisure Guide, 'North York Moors', 1987, AA Publishing.

I. Carstairs, 'The North York Moors National Park', 1987, Webb & Bower.

M. Colbeck, 'Village Yorkshire', 1987, B. T. Batsford Ltd.

M. Sugden, 'Yorkshire Moors and Dales', 1987, The Pevensey Press.

M. Williams, 'Witches in Old North Yorkshire', 1987, Hutton Press Ltd.

R. H. Hayes, 'Old Roads and Pannierways in North East Yorkshire', 1988, North York Moors National Park.

D. A. Spratt and B. J. D. Harrison, 'The North York Moors Landscape Heritage', 1989, David & Charles.

J. Tindale, 'The Changing Moors', 1990, Dalesman.

Peter N. Walker, 'Folk Tales from the North York Moors', 1990, Robert Hale.

R. Talbot and R. Whiteman 'The Yorkshire Moors and Dales', 1991, Weidenfeld & Nicolson.

North Yorkshire Federations of Women's Institutes, 'The North Yorkshire Village Book', 1991, Countryside Books.

L. Graham, 'The Crosses of the North Yorkshire Moors', 1993, North Riding Publishing.

Staniforth, 'Geology of the North York Moors', 1993, North York Moors National Park.

E. Ogilvie and A. Sleightholme, 'An Illustrated Guide to the Crosses on the North Yorkshire Moors', 1994, The Village Green Press.

AA / Ordnance Survey Leisure Guide, 'North York Moors', 1996, AA Publishing.

M. Reid, 'The Inn Way...to the Yorkshire Dales', 1997, InnWay Publications

North York Moors National Park Authority 'Management Plan', 1998

North York Moors National Park Authority 'Measuring Change', 1998

M. Reid, 'The Inn Way...to the English Lake District', 1998, InnWay Publications

North York Moors National Park Authority 'Annual Report', 1998/9

R. Protz (Editor), 'Good Beer Guide 2000', 2000, CAMRA

J. S. Fletcher, 'Nooks & Corners of Yorkshire', date unknown, Eveleigh Nash.

S. P. B. Mais & T. Stephenson (Editors), 'Lovely Britain', date unknown. Odhams Press.

W. Andrews, 'Picturesque Yorkshire', date unknown, Valentine & Sons Ltd.

Top: Helmsley. © Mark Reid

Middle: Hutton le Hole. © Peter Neusser

Bottom: St Gregory's Minster. © Mark Reid

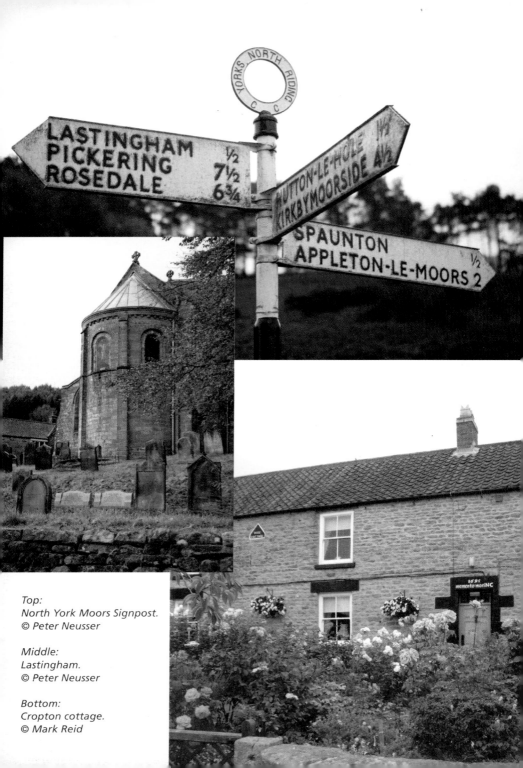

Top:
North York Moors Signpost.
© Peter Neusser

Middle:
Lastingham.
© Peter Neusser

Bottom:
Cropton cottage.
© Mark Reid

Top: Newton Dale. © Mark Reid

Middle: North Yorkshire Moors
        Railway. © Peter Neusser

Bottom: Levisham Station. © Mark Reid

Top: Birch Hall Inn. © Mark Reid

Middle: Elvis on Two Howes Rigg. © Mark Reid

Bottom: Killing Nab Scar. © Mark Reid

Top: Beggar's Bridge. © Mark Reid

Middle: Arncliffe Wood. © Mark Reid

Bottom: Great Fryup Dale. © Mark Reid

Top: Rosedale. © Mark Reid

Middle: Moorland Stone. © Peter Neusser

Bottom: Bransdale. © Mark Reid

Top: Hawnby Fireplace. © Peter Neusser

Middle: Bransdale Mill. © Mark Reid

Bottom: Hawnby © Peter Neusser

Top: *Arden Hall.* © Mark Reid

Middle: *Rievaulx Abbey.* © Peter Neusser

Bottom: *Hambleton Hills.* © Mark Reid

The Inn Way...*to the North York Moors*

LOG BOOK
· ·

"Drinking in the scenery"

✦

Visit as many of the thirty-one inns along *The Inn Way... to the North York Moors* as possible and keep a record of your progress with this Log Book.

Send your completed Log Book to the address below to receive your free 'Inn Way' certificate (please include an A4 SAE as well as your name and address; we will return this Log Book with your certificate). Photocopies of this Log Book will not be accepted.

'The Inn Way' Merchandise and Gifts
If you would like to purchase an 'Inn Way' certificate then please write to us for a copy of 'The Inn Way' brochure, or visit our website.

We produce a range of walking guidebooks as well as a selection of quality merchandise and gift items including 'Inn Way' branded outdoor fleeces, polo shirts, performance T-shirts, glass beer tankards, fabric badges plus much more...

InnWay Publications
102 LEEDS ROAD
HARROGATE
HG2 8HB

www.innway.co.uk

LOG BOOK

. . . .

Day One   Date / Time of Visit / Remarks

1.   Feathers, Helmsley   . . . .

2.   Black Swan, Helmsley   . . . .

3.   Crown Inn, Helmsley   . . . .

4.   Royal Oak, Helmsley   . . . .

5.   Feversham Arms Hotel,
     Helmsley   . . . .

6.   Star Inn, Harome   . . . .

7.   Plough Inn, Wombleton   . . . .

8.   Plough Inn, Fadmoor   . . . .

9.   Royal Oak Inn, Gillamoor   . . . .

10. Crown, Hutton-le-Hole   . . . .

Day Two

11. Blacksmiths Arms, Lastingham   . . . .

12. New Inn, Cropton   . . . .

13. White Swan,
     Newton-on-Rawcliffe   . . . .

14. Horseshoe Inn, Levisham   . . . .

Day Three

15. Spout Bar, Mallyan Hotel,
    Goathland

    . . . .

16. Goathland Hotel, Goathland

    . . . .

17. Inn on the Moor, Goathland

    . . . .

18. Birch Hall Inn, Beck Hole

    . . . .

19. Horseshoe Hotel, Egton Bridge

    . . . .

20. Postgate Inn, Egton Bridge

    . . . .

Day Four

21. Arncliffe Arms, Glaisdale

    . . . .

22. The Moon and Sixpence,
    Glaisdale *(closed)*

    . . . .

23. The Mitre Tavern,
    Glaisdale *(closed)*

    . . . .

24. Board Inn, Lealholm

    . . . .

25. Milburn Arms Hotel,
    Rosedale Abbey

    . . . .

26. White Horse Farm Inn,
    Rosedale Abbey

    . . . .

27. Coach House Inn,
    Rosedale Abbey

    . . . .

Day Five

28. Feversham Arms, Church Houses . . . .

29. Sun Inn, Bilsdale   . . . .

30. Inn at Hawnby, Hawnby   . . . .

Day Six

31. Hare Inn, Scawton   . . . .

Addendum: The Pheasant, Harome

◆

Name . . . .
(as it is to appear on the certificate)

Address . . . .

. . . .

Date completed. . . . .

Don't forget the SAE